Hearing the Voice of the Child

The Representation of Children's Interests in Public Law Proceedings

Edited by
Maria Ruegger

Russell House Publishing

First published in 2001 by:
Russell House Publishing Ltd.
4 St. George's House
Uplyme Road
Lyme Regis
Dorset DT7 3LS

Tel: 01297-443948
Fax: 01297-442722
e-mail: help@russellhouse.co.uk

British Library Cataloguing-in-publication Data:
A catalogue record for this book is available from the British Library.

ISBN: 1-898924-82-1

Typeset by TW Typesetting, Plymouth, Devon
Printed by Bell and Bain, Glasgow

Russell House Publishing

Is a group of social work, probation, education and youth and community work practitioners and academics working in collaboration with a professional publishing team.
Our aim is to work closely with the field to produce innovative and valuable materials to help managers, trainers, practitioners and students.
We are keen to receive feedback on publications and new ideas for future projects.

Contents

About the Authors

His Honour Judge Roger Connor was formerly a solicitor in general litigation practice. In 1983 he was appointed a metropolitan stipendiary magistrate and (in addition to the court's criminal jurisdiction) sat in the Domestic Proceedings and Juvenile Courts. As a chairman of Juvenile Courts he dealt with applications for care orders under the pre Children Act 1989 legislation. He has been a circuit judge since 1991 and is the Designated Family Judge for Hertfordshire and also Liaison Judge for Buckinghamshire.

Julia Isikwe Hughes qualified as a social worker in 1990. She has a MSc in Social Work, for which she undertook research into Black children in Care. She also obtained a postgraduate certificate in Inter Cultural Therapy and an Advanced Award in Social Work. Julia is an experienced practice teacher and currently acts as an external assessor for the North London Practice Teachers Consortium, and as a practice assessor for the Child Care Award. She predominantly worked as a self-employed Guardian ad Litem for the Surrey and South London Panels prior to the establishment of CAFCASS. Julia also undertakes teaching, training and consultancy work on issues relating to Black children in care. She has published *Implications of the Lawrence Inquiry and Macpherson Report to Guardians ad Litem* in the March 2000, Vol 10, Issue 1 edition of Seen and Heard.

Gillian Norris qualified as a social worker in 1971. She has specialised in work with children throughout her career, working in a number of different settings including social services, a women's refuge, a school for children with special educational needs and paediatrics. Early in her professional life she formed a special interest in analytical psychology and play therapy and she has continued to develop her knowledge and expertise in this area, much of which she brings to her work with children as a Guardian ad Litem. She has also worked in mental health psycho-therapy services. Gillian has been a Guardian ad Litem on the Hertfordshire panel since 1985 and has a special interest in communicating with children through direct work.

Arran Poyser joined the Department of Health(DH) in 1985 as a social services inspector. He was closely involved with preparation for, and implementation of, the Children Act 1989. He had policy lead for the GALRO service from 1991 until early 2001. His other policy responsibilities have included domestic violence, the UN Convention on the Rights of the Child, care proceedings and care plans, and the interface between the DH, the family courts and the Lord Chancellor's Department. He was closely involved with proposals for a unified court welfare service which led to the 1998 Consultation Paper and follow-up work. From November 1999, he was seconded to the CAFCASS Implementation Project. He now works for HM Magistrates' Courts Service Inspectorate where he is in charge of inspection arrangements for CAFCASS across England and Wales.

Vivienne Reed has a social work background in childcare and has, for the last eight years, combined both management and practitioner roles. She has held the post of manager of the Hertfordshire Guardian ad Litem and Reporting Officer Panel and has practiced as both a social work consultant and a Guardian ad Litem for the Inner and North London Panel. Her most recent research undertaken for the award of M.B.A, focussed on organizational management, with a particular emphasis on mentoring, coaching, professional development groups and appraisal. Her consultancy interests include Part 8 inquiries, complex complaint investigations, and training. She has also undertaken service reviews and service specifications for organizations undergoing change and has had published several papers on organizational management. Vivienne has a particular interest in and experience of working with refugee children.

Maria Ruegger is a Senior lecturer in Social Work at De Montfort University. She has also been a Guardian ad Litem on the Hertfordshire Panel of Guardians ad Litem and Reporting Officers since 1985. Maria qualified as a social worker in 1978 and worked in the fields of mental health and childcare. Her recent research interests include Children's Perspectives of the Guardian ad Litem Service and Mentoring in General Practice, and she has published widely in these areas. Since 1985 when she took up a teaching post at the university she has maintained strong links with practice, both as a social work consultant and as a Guardian ad Litem. Maria has acted as an appraiser for the Surrey, Berkshire, Essex and Inner and North London Panels of Guardians ad Litem and Reporting Officers and as a consultant to Surrey, Essex, Hampshire and Hertfordshire Panels of Guardians ad Litem and Reporting Officers.

Sarah Stevens has been a practising solicitor for 20 years. She has specialised in family law for 15 years, in representing children for 10 years and is a member of the Law Society Children Panel. Sarah recently completed a postgraduate course in Child Studies at Kings College, London. She has developed a particular interest and expertise in the representation of middle and teenage children whose interests are usually considered by the adults involved with them, but who are themselves excluded from the court processes.

Penelope Wood is a practising barrister. She qualified as a solicitor in 1972 and specialised in public and private children's law as a member of the Law Society Children Panel. In 1999 she transferred to the Bar. She was a magistrate for several years and sat on the Juvenile Panel. She acted on behalf of the children in *X v. Bedfordshire* in the Care Proceedings. She initiated and had conduct, on the instructions of the Official Solicitor, of their personal injury litigation through the English Courts. She is also instructed by the Official Solicitor and in respect of the children's application to the European Court of Human Rights which challenges the local authority public policy immunity created by the House of Lords decision in *X v. Bedfordshire*.

Acknowledgements

Grateful thanks are due to a number of people who have assisted in the creation of this book. Ann Wheal generously gave of her time and was most helpful in the outline planning and early development of the ideas upon which the book came to be based. Gwynneth Boswell, a Senior Research Fellow at De Montfort University, and Sarah Stevens, a solicitor in private practice and herself a contributor to this book, took on the demanding task of critical reading, and their astute insights are reflected within these pages. Geoffrey Mann of Russell House Publishing, Vivienne Reed, the manager of the Hertfordshire Guardian ad litem Panel, Elizabeth Sullivan, a Senior Research Fellow of De Montfort University, my husband Fred and my sons Carl and Josh, all provided much needed encouragement and support when energy levels flagged and the task seemed impossible. My thanks are of course due to all of the authors, each of whom has taken time from their demanding professional lives to share their insights and experience of working in the complex and demanding field of public law.

Finally, I am indebted to my colleagues on the Hertfordshire Panel of Guardians ad litem, and to the children with whom I have worked who must remain unidentified in order that their privacy be respected, all of whom have contributed to the ideas that led to this book being written.

Maria Ruegger

Foreword

I think this is the first time that I have been asked to write a piece of prose such as that which I now attempt. Having been persuaded to do so I can tell you that I was not looking forward to the task; and for a number of reasons.

To begin with I would have to read the book. Those of us involved in the child care system, both lawyers and other professionals, have to read so much in the course of our day-to-day work that one can do without having to read the quantity of material that you will see now follows this page. I hope and believe that one attribute of a forward to a book of any worth is that it should be honest, indeed one might say even frank. So, frankly speaking, what I have to say is that having been somewhat less than enthusiastic I am now glad that I allowed myself to be persuaded to this task. Quite simply, I have enjoyed doing it.

Those of us in The System have read so much about the subject that were it not for our steadfast and unremitting Commitment to the work we would be tempted to think that we had nothing more to learn. Of course it is the case that some sections of this book prompt no surprises but even those sections are worth reading to remind us of familiar things, re-cast from a slightly different angle. However there was much that I have found stimulating and, dare I say it, making me think. The thoughts were always positive even if sometimes I was not enthused by what was proposed, although equally sometimes I was. Let me give some examples.

I particularly enjoyed reading Chapter 3 on the role of the guardian and wondered with the author what could be done to avail ourselves of the benefits of the involvement of experts from other disciplines without incurring what realistically one has to accept becomes an often inordinate delay.

In this same chapter I questioned whether, as the author suggests, it really is right for the system and for the children involved for a guardian usually to instruct the same solicitor or one from a very small circle of solicitors. I wondered whether the stimulus of professionals, strangers to each other, might produce a less cosy but intellectually more rigorous approach to a particular case. I was pleased to see that the author of Chapter 6 recognised that one consequence of a child being able to instruct a solicitor direct was that his or her instructions had to be followed to the letter even if contrary to what the advocate perceived to be the best interests of the child or the family taken as a whole. However I found myself in total disagreement with the suggestion that there is no essential difference between representing a competent child and an adult. Certainly I have never ever shared the experience of this author and heard a child 'give evidence and be cross-examined'. And so on.

As the title of the book suggests, there are tensions in the role of all professionals in the system. Most certainly the voice of the child must be heard; but equally the professional's informed and personal assessment of the child's best interests must be advocated. The two are by no means always congruent. What I have liked about this book is that it approaches a range of problems and of situations from the standpoint of particular professionals. The tasks involved can never be easy but I have felt that my own approach is the better for my having read the book and thought about points that it raised which either I hadn't thought about before or hadn't seen in quite the same light. I think you will find the same.

The Honourable Mr Justice Johnson,
Family Division Liaison Judge for the South Eastern Circuit.

Introduction

The purpose in writing this book is to encourage professionals in the field of family law, whose work brings them into contact with children, to think about and debate, perhaps from the children's point of view, some of the issues that have arisen in the representation of children's interests in public law proceedings, and to consider some of the processes involved.

The opportunity to reflect on what Children's Guardians do, why they do it, how they do it and how they can improve their practice is particularly important with the unification of those separate organisations that have historically been involved with children who become the subjects of civil proceedings. Whilst initially Court Welfare Officers, Guardians and case workers from the Official Solicitor's department are continuing to work within their own specialisms, the intention is that in time, staff who join the unified service, the Children and Family Court Advisory and Support Service (CAFCASS), will acquire the necessary skills to enable them to take on all of the work referred. It is my hope that this book will be a contribution to the professional development of all those who are involved in public law proceedings.

In addition to those who work within CAFCASS, there are other professional groups whose work involves them closely with children during court proceedings, and who are likely to find much of the material in this text relevant to the tasks in which they engage. These groups include those who act as expert witnesses, for example paediatricians, psychiatrists, and psychologists, solicitors and barristers who act for children. Social workers who specialise in child protection may find that particular topics will be of interest to them. Many of the experiences of these children are likely to be shared by those whose family circumstances bring them within the wider orbit of the civil courts. Finally, there are others who have less direct involvement with children, such as the judiciary, policy makers and those responsible for the organisation and delivery of national and local services, yet whose daily tasks have long-term consequences for some children. They may be interested to learn something of how children experience the impact of their decisions, and of the experiences of those whose task it is to hear their stories first hand.

This book deals with the current legal system and the framework for professional practice in the representation of children within public law proceedings. Chapters 1 to 4 have been written by Maria Ruegger, who also edits the book. Maria is a practising Guardian ad litem, in addition to being a lecturer in social work and a researcher. She brings to this book her understanding of the complexities of the roles that professionals working in the arena of family law must undertake, and the difficulties that can often be encountered in translating theoretical ideals into practice.

Chapter 1 introduces some definitions and deals with the changes taking place in 2001.

Chapter 2 explores in detail those aspects of research, law, and current thinking that combine to produce a framework for the knowledge base that underpins the Guardian ad litem's investigation. It is particularly concerned with the 'no order principle' and the legal requirement to ensure that any orders made in respect of the child leave them in a better position than they would have been if no order had been made. This provokes an examination of what the state has to offer as an alternative to family care, and current government plans to improve the quality of life for children in state care are discussed. In Chapter 3 the role of the Guardian ad litem is explored in detail, and in Chapter 4, examples of children's experiences as gleaned from recent research are described.

Gillian Norris, a Guardian on the Hertfordshire panel for 17 years, shares with readers in Chapter 5 some of the considerable skills and expertise she has acquired in direct work with children who are the subjects of court proceedings.

Julia Hughes, a Guardian on the Surrey and Inner and North London Panels, in Chapter 6 explores the meaning and importance of issues of identity, race and culture as they relate to black children, and examines the contentious area of balancing needs arising from race with other needs, such as those arising from emotional and psychological attachments the black child may have formed with white carers.

In Chapter 7 Judge Roger Connor, a senior Family Court judge, discusses the roles of expert witnesses in proceedings, their use and mis-use, and gives a personal judicial perspective on this complex subject.

In Chapter 8 Sarah Stevens, an experienced family lawyer and Children Panel member who is regularly instructed by Guardians on behalf on children, writes about the difficult issue of deciding which children should be allowed to instruct their lawyers directly.

Vivienne Reed, an experienced Guardian who has also managed the Hertfordshire Guardian ad litem Panel for eight years, discusses in Chapter 9 some of the complex issues historically linked to the boundaries of the Guardian's role and with examples, highlights aspects of good practice and considers the likely benefits and possible disadvantages for Guardians in joining CAFCASS.

In Chapter 10 Penelope Wood, a barrister who specialises in family law, considers the effect of the implementation (on 2 October 2000) of the Human Rights Act 1998 on children involved in civil proceedings. The Human Rights Act is likely to have a significant impact on all who work within the field of both public and private law.

In the final chapter, Arran Poyser, Cheif Inspector of CAFCASS at H.M. Magistrates' Courts Service Inspectorate, writes about the detail of the changes that have come about with the birth of CAFCASS in April 2001. Arran has been the civil servant responsible for the Guardian service, and has been closely involved with the design and establishment of CAFCASS.

This book then covers the role of the Guardian in general whilst also raising some of the complexities, and highlighting some of the privileges, of working with children who become subjects of family law proceedings. It raises issues to do with best practice, at a time when there is much opportunity for professional development, given the amalgamation of the three services which have traditionally worked with children who come before the courts in civil proceedings. It is hoped that discussion and debate will also be stimulated amongst others who are not directly involved in CAFCASS, but who have a vested interest in improving the services available to children at a point in their lives which is full of uncertainty and anxiety, whether this be as a result of private or public proceedings.

List of Abbreviations

ABSWAP	Association of Black Social Workers and Allied Professionals
ACPC	Area Child Protection Committee
BAAF	British Association of Adoption and Fostering
CAFCASS	Children and Family Court Advisory and Support Service
FLRA	Family Law Reform Act [1969 and 1987]
FPR	Family Proceedings Rules
GAL	Guardian ad litem
GCSE	General Certificate of Secondary Education
GNVQ	General National Vocational Qualification
HRA	Human Rights Act 1998
ISS	International Social Services
LAC	Looked after Children
NSPCC	National Society for Prevention of Cruelty to Children
SFLA	Solicitors Family Law Association

1 The Children Involved in Family Law Proceedings

Maria Ruegger

Introduction

Statistics supplied by the Department of Health in *The Children Act Report, 1995-9*, show that in 1998, 70,709 orders were made by the courts within private law proceedings and 15,704 orders were made within public law proceedings. As it is not uncommon for there to be more than one order in respect of each child, the number of children involved in both private and public law proceedings is likely to be less than the total number of orders. The prime concern of this book is with those children involved in public law proceedings. Only these children have 'party' status as of right, which means the right to be represented in legal proceedings. This introductory chapter outlines the key differences between private and public law proceedings, and also between the welfare services that have evolved to ensure that children in civil proceedings have their views and interests placed before the court alongside those of other parties. Until April 2001 these services were entirely separate but they have since been combined into a new organisation, The Children and Family Court Advisory and Support Service (CAFCASS). How this new service is intended to operate is briefly described.

Private Law Proceedings

Most children who are the subjects of private law proceedings are those whose parents are in the process of divorcing. When initiating proceedings the parent seeking divorce completes a form setting out the proposed arrangements as to the child's accommodation, education, care, financial support, and contact with the non-residential parent. There is however, no provision for setting out the child's own views, no obligation for the parent to ascertain them or discuss the proposals and no requirement to indicate whether the child is in agreement with the proposed arrangements. Accordingly if there is no dispute between the parents there is little likelihood that the court will be aware of the wishes and feelings of the child. If the parents are in dispute, or the arrangements are plainly inadequate, the court will appoint a Court Welfare Officer to carry out an independent investigation into the circumstances of the case. In rare cases, and where the court believes the child may be at risk of significant harm, the local authority will be directed to investigate whether they should start public law proceedings. If they conclude they do not need to, then the court can take no further protective steps to safeguard the child's welfare.

Where a Court Welfare Officer is appointed they will usually see both parents separately, and the children, both on their own and together with their parents. They may also make limited enquiries of the children's school and of other adults with particular and relevant knowledge of them. The emphasis is on assisting the parents to reach agreement. Where agreement is achieved the court's role is at an end. There will be no hearing or other investigation into the appropriateness of the resolution. The underlying assumptions are that parents do not stop being good parents upon divorce, and that they will continue to make responsible decisions for the care of their children.

Children are not normally parties in private law proceedings and thus do not have access to legal advice and representation in their own right, the right to attend court or to express their views to the court. A very small percentage of children will be represented, either by being considered sufficiently mature by the court to be granted party status and participate directly, or by the appointment of the Official Solicitor to represent them where the court considers their interests require this, and the Official Solicitor agrees to act. The majority either don't know of these possibilities or, even if they did, would not have the knowledge and skills required to access them unless help were provided. This, of course, may change following the implementation of the Human Rights Act 1998, see Chapter 10, and implimentation of the proposed changes to the court rules that considerably extend the duties of those undertaking welfare reporting (see Chapter 11).

Accordingly in the current system, children in private law proceedings are largely dependent on their parents and, where appointed, Court Welfare Officers, to ascertain their wishes and relay them to the court. They do not have any right of appeal if they do not like the final decisions made by the court about which parent they should live with, the nature of the contact they can have with the non resident parent or any other aspects of their post divorce care.

Ruxton expresses the view that:

> *Children are among the most powerless of social groups and often have very limited opportunities to be involved in key decisions which affect them. Recognising their competence and valuing their contribution, individually and collectively, is a crucial prerequisite for creating a dynamic, participative society. This means respecting the individuality of children who are not merely dependent on adults, but also social actors in their own right.*

> Ruxton, 1995.

Private law proceedings constitute one such area where children are often powerless.

Public Law Proceedings

Public law proceedings are those in which the court's authority, to interfere in what would normally be considered private family business, is sought by the state. The state must demonstrate that the child has suffered, or is likely to suffer, significant harm, and that this is attributable to the care they receive from their parents. The state carries out these functions through social workers who are employed by local authorities. It is the responsibility of social workers to investigate circumstances in which children are thought to be suffering harm, and, in the first instance, to provide families with services, and support, aimed at assisting them in the care and upbringing of their children.

The benefits to children of being cared for within their families are central to the philosophy underlying the legislative framework of public law proceedings within the Children Act 1989. Children who are cared for by the state are known to do less well than those brought up in families, in a number of important respects such as health, education and employment (see for example Bamford *et al.*, 1987, and Jackson, 1998: these are discussed in some detail in Chapter 2). It is for this reason that the Children Act 1989 reflects the need to support families in the care and upbringing of their children, section 17 (1) (b)), and that, even where it can be shown that the child has suffered significant harm as a result of the care provided by their family, the court must be satisfied that to make an order in respect of the child is better than making no order at all.

If efforts on the part of the local authority to assist parents to provide a good enough standard of care for their children have failed, or in circumstances where the harm is thought to be so great that it would be inappropriate for the child to remain within the family, the local authority can apply to the court for orders which allow it to make important decisions about the child, notwithstanding parental objections. These decisions cover such matters as with whom the child should live throughout their childhood, whom they should see and how often they should see them.

Key Differences between the Representation of Children in Public and Private Law Proceedings

In public law proceedings children have party status. Courts appoint Guardians ad litem, from 1 April 2001 known generically as officers of CAFCASS and as children's guardians in respect of much of the work that they currently undertake, to assist the child in this regard. Guardians instruct solicitors on behalf of the child, and are also responsible for ascertaining the views of the child, relaying them to the court and for keeping the child informed throughout the proceedings. Guardians usually have a social work background in child protection, and have specialised in the area of court work. They are regarded by the courts as experts in their field. Courts rely heavily on the advice and recommendations of the Guardian who, in

Table 1: Types of law proceedings as affecting children, before 2001

Civil Law			Criminal Law (not the concern of this book)	
Private law		*Public law ie, the state interferes in what would normally be private family affairs*	*Private*	*Public*
Court Welfare Officer	Official Solicitor	Guardian ad litem		
Children not normally parties in private law, therefore no right to attend court or to representation except where parents divorcing and dispute or arrangements inadequate, court may appoint *Court Welfare Officer* to investigate	Certain limited High Court cases, child is represented by *Official Solicitor*, those principally relevant to this book concern: 1. Cases where there is legal or moral complexity central to children's welfare, and court feels child's best interests require independent representation 2. Child who wishes to make own application to court, but not mature enough to appoint own solicitor	Children have party status; Courts appoint *Guardians ad litem* to assist child, e.g. where it is thought that a child's care is neglectful or abusive and that the child may be at risk of significant harm and the local authority initiate care proceedings	Private criminal proceedings not usual	Almost all criminal proceedings brought by Crown Prosecution Service, on behalf of the state

addition to reporting to the court the wishes and views of children, is required to give their own view as to the child's best interests.

Generally children within private law proceedings will only have a voice when their parents are in dispute, and then only indirectly through the Court Welfare Officer's report. Court Welfare Officers, known now as Children and Family Reporters, endeavour to ascertain and relay to the court the wishes and feelings of children and will make recommendations as to which proposed outcome is in their best interests. They have not traditionally been permitted to seek legal representation on behalf of the child. As with their Guardian colleagues, courts generally accept the opinions of Court Welfare Officers when making decisions about which parent the children should reside with and the frequency and nature of contact with the other parent.

Thus, the Guardian ad litem and the Court Welfare Officer have had similar tasks in that they both have had a duty to relay the children's wishes and feelings to the court, and to give their own recommendation as to the

The Children Involved in Family Law Proceedings 5

Table 2: Differences between representation of children in public and private law proceedings (powers of child and representative) before 2001

Private law— *Court Welfare Officer:*	*Private law/Public law—* *Official Solicitor:*	*Public law—* *Guardian ad litem:*
Part of Probation Service		Service managed by local authority
Usually has background in Probation service or in the fields of adult and/or juvenille crime	Officer of court	Usually has background in social work and child protection, usually expert in their field
If parents in dispute, CWO can relay child's wishes to court and make recommendations in best interests of child	Will report on child's wishes and make recommendations as to best interests	Is channel of communication between court and child and makes recommendations as to best interests
May **not** instruct solicitors on behalf of child	Will represent the child	Almost always will instruct solicitors on behalf of child
Courts generally accept opinions of CWO when making decision's about child's welfare	Courts rely on advice from Official Solicitor	Courts rely on advice and recommendations of Guardian
	Scope of enquiries not usually so far reaching as those of Guardian ad litem. Functions are similar although not identical to Guardians ad litem	Traditionally been more proactive in proceedings than court welfare officers (e.g. appraising local authorities work with family, looking at future plans)
		Likely to see child's extended family network, teachers etc.
	Can ask the court to appoint expert witnesses (e.g. child psychiatrists) to assist in assessing child	Can ask the court to appoint expert witnesses (e.g. child psychiatrists) to assist in assessing child
Sees all papers and reports	Sees all papers and reports	Sees all papers and reports and LA files
Not a key player in court hearings, may only attend court to be examined on contents on their reports	May file evidence, call and cross-examine witnesses in support of his recommendation. Key player in court hearings	Key player in court hearings, conducts case for child, instructs solicitor to cross examine witnesses, call evidence etc.
Does not automatically have status of expert witness		May be expert witness, with power to address court, having heard all evidence
Has no right of appeal if outcome is not in accordance with their recommendations	Has right of appeal if recommendation not accepted by Court	Has right of appeal if recommendation not accepted by Court

best outcome. However, the Guardians have traditionally been much more involved in the proceedings in that they have a proactive role and a wider investigative brief. For example, in addition to considering the plans put forward by the parents, they appraised the work that the local authority might have been engaged in with the family in the past with a view to avoiding the need to take proceedings, and also looked at the future plans of the local authority for the particular child, assuming its application was successful.

Guardians, are also likely to see members of the child's extended family network, their teachers, and others intimately involved with them and their family. The Guardian can ask the court to appoint expert witnesses, such as child psychiatrists and psychologists, to assist them in their assessment of the needs and best interests of the child. In contrast, the Court Welfare Officers' investigations have traditionally been limited to seeing the children once with each of their parents and once alone. The Guardian, unlike the Court Welfare Officer, is a key player in court hearings. Whilst both see all the papers and reports filed in the proceedings, the Guardian conducts the case on behalf of the child (save where the child disagrees with their Guardian and is sufficiently mature to instruct their solicitor direct). They thus instruct the solicitor to advocate the child's views, to cross examine witnesses and call evidence to support their opinions as to the best interests of the child. They also have the opportunity as an expert witness to address the court having first heard all the evidence. Finally, they can decide whether to lodge an appeal if the court's decision is not in accord with their own view as to the child's best interests.

Court Welfare Officers also attend court hearings, but only for the purpose of being examined on the contents of their reports. While considerable respect is accorded to their views, Court Welfare Officers do not automatically have the status of an expert witness. They do not normally stay for the evidence put forward by the parents or the court's decision (but could do), and they have no right of appeal if the outcome is not in accordance with their recommendations.

The Official Solicitor's Department

The Department of the Official Solicitor also represents a small number of children, primarily in proceedings in the High Court in certain limited and exceptional situations where there are issues of moral or legal complexity. Those most relevant to this discussion are cases falling into two categories. Those involving children whose parents are engaged in litigation concerning them, and where the court feels that the safeguarding of their best interests requires independent representation rather than the preparation of a Court Welfare Officer's report, and those of children who the court has agreed should make their own applications, but who are not deemed sufficiently mature to instruct a solicitor themselves. The Official Solicitor's role is similar to that of a Guardian although the scope of their enquiries might not need to be so far reaching. They will report on the child's wishes and feelings but also make a recommendation as to best interests. They will arrange representation, usually instruct experts, file evidence, call and cross-examine witnesses in support of their recommendation, and can appeal if it is not accepted by the court.

The Launch of the 'Children and Family Court Advisory and Support Service'

Until April 2001, the services charged with representing children's interests in civil proceedings were totally separate. The Court Welfare service came under the umbrella of the Probation service, whilst the Guardian ad litem service was managed by the local authority, albeit at arms length from its childcare department. The Official Solicitor's Department is based in London and has a number of responsibilities, one of which is to represent children; only their childrens service is affected by CAFCASS.

All three services, the Court Welfare service, the Guardian ad litem service and the Official Solicitor's children's service, were combined on 1 April 2001 to form the Child and Family Court Advisory and Support Service (CAFCASS). However, this book mostly uses the terms prevalent before 2001 to help in explaining the background to the new combined service. Though the discussion may be about the Guardian ad litem and the Guardian service, the consideration is of the future for work with children in the field of public law.

Since the outset, the intention of CAFCASS has been that the services operate in a similar way to past practice, although eventually this may change. Guardians ad litem, Court Welfare Officers and case workers of the Official Solicitor's Departments are all now known as officers of CAFCASS. When the court decides it needs the services of a CAFCASS officer, the manager of the local CAFCASS team allocates the case to the person who is most likely to be able to carry out the required tasks. Children who are involved in private law proceedings have an officer who was previously a Court Welfare Officer and do not automatically have party status. Children who are the subjects of public law proceedings continue to have party status and have officers who were previously Guardians ad litem appointed to assist them. Similarly work which would have been allocated to the Official Solicitor's Department is distributed amongst those appropriate staff. Once an officer has been chosen, that information is passed to court staff and the officer's name appears on the Order appointing them to the particular case.

Traditionally the Court Welfare service has been less well resourced than the Guardian service and the Official Solicitor's Department. For example, Court Welfare Officers took on many more cases and wrote many more reports than did Guardians and, unlike Guardians, they could not appoint experts to assist them in determining the child's best interests, or obtain legal representation for children. In many areas Court Welfare Officers worked to specific targets in an attempt to ensure that the enormous volume of work was allocated and completed within a reasonable timeframe. The Guardian service on the other hand worked in a system much less geared to levels of resources, in which each Guardian made their own decision about the demands of a specific case and allocated time accordingly. Legal representation was almost always available to the Guardian, as was expertise in a specific field, although subject to the approval of the court. Case workers in the Official Solicitors Department, like their Guardian colleagues, have traditionally had access both to legal representation and to expert opinion on behalf of children. Concern has been expressed that, over time, achieving equal service provision for all children who become subjects in civil proceedings will result in the dilution of the service to those who become subjects in public law proceedings. It is the hope of the author that, instead, the interests of children in private law proceedings will receive more attention, and that services to them will, in the long run, be enhanced as a result of the formation of CAFCASS.

Do Children Need a Guardian as well as a Solicitor?

It is, of course, reasonable to explore the question of whether, and to what extent, children benefit from the system which allows their views and interests to be represented through a Guardian and a legal representative within public law proceedings. Is there a case instead for allowing children the right to instruct their lawyers directly, attend court and participate fully in proceedings in the same way as other parties do? The child's 'best interests' are the subject of a good deal of debate, argument and thought. Jim Richards when commenting on a paper by Freeman (1994) reflects:

> ... *that to give children complete autonomy, as some of the child liberationists would advocate, would make it more likely for them not to be able to exercise effective autonomy as adults. He (Freeman) also argues that the goal that we wish to achieve for children becoming adults is rational independence and that although in growing up we have to make mistakes, so that we can learn from our experiences, no rational child would wish to make such serious mistakes as would jeopardise their future as happy, competent adults. The difficulty is in what circumstances we, as adults, impose our will to prevent mistakes being made. It involves paternalism which Freeman warns us is a double edged sword and that those who exercise constraints must do so in such a way as to enable children to develop their capacities.*
>
> Richards, 1995.

In order to establish a view about the child's ability to exercise autonomy, one has to consider their current capacity to understand their situation, the consequences of the different outcomes and the effect on their emotional well-being of their involvement in any court proceedings. The balance between children's rights and others' perspectives of the child's best interests are particularly difficult in areas such as:

- The potential future risk to the child.
- The measures which can be put in place to ameliorate these.
- The advisability of a return home versus the perils and pitfalls of the 'care system' particularly for the older child.
- The pressure the child may feel from other family members to take a particular position.
- The particularly sensitive issue of loyalty to parents, whatever the circumstances which led to care proceedings being initiated.

In practice it is the task of the Guardian ad litem together with the child's solicitor to undertake this balancing exercise, although the responsibility lies with the solicitor in determining whether the child can give their own instructions directly, without the assistance of the Guardian.

Children who are considered by their solicitors as competent, are able to part company from their Guardian or Advisor and instruct their solicitor independently. Available research suggests that few children do instruct solicitors directly. Evidence from a number of recent studies (Clarke (1995); Masson and Oakley (1999); Ruegger (2001)), suggests that the option of direct representation is not something which is taken up as often as one might expect taking other factors into consideration. The complex reasons for this are explored by Sarah Stevens in Chapter 8 of this book. (In situations where children do give their own instructions, the Guardian either represents themselves or, if the proceedings are complicated, will instruct a solicitor to represent them in their own right.)

Judith Timms, when discussing the role of the Guardian ad litem presenting the case regarding the child's welfare and the children's panel solicitor acting as an advocate for the child, indicates that, in situations where both are working well together, there may be nothing left for the child to say to the court. Yet in studies conducted by Clarke (1992), Ruegger (2001) and Masson and Oakley (1999) significant numbers of children expressed the wish to be more involved in court hearings and to be present in court. These children included those who were satisfied that their wishes and feelings had been heard by the judiciary through their Guardians and solicitors. What may be important for children is that, if they wish, they should be active participants in the decision-making process that will affect their lives. The extent to which children feel that the tension between rights and best interests is fairly balanced, is the subject of Chapter 4, which reports the findings of research on children's perspectives.

It was feared by many practitioners that this tandem model of representation of children in public law proceedings would be lost with the establishment of CAFCASS, due to the expense involved. That it has been retained is due to the overwhelming support from practitioners and the judiciary for its continuation, and this in itself suggests that the benefits of having both solicitors and guardians involved outweigh the disadvantages. That it seems likely to become available to those children who require it in private law proceedings is to be welcomed.

2 Social Work Practice with Children involved in Family Law Proceedings: A Guardian's Assessment of the Child's Best Interests

Maria Ruegger

Introduction

This second chapter explores the wider context of social work practice with children and families. It looks at the factors which influence Guardians' thinking when making decisions about whether, and how far, the state should intervene in those situations where children may be suffering harm as a result of inadequate parenting. The circumstances of the children who come before the courts in family law proceedings are described, as are the kinds of risks posed to them by their families, and the risks posed to them by the care system itself. There is often a difficult balance to be achieved in deciding whether the risks for a particular child are likely to be greater within the care system or within their family. It is, of course, the case that for some children, the risk is too great for them to remain in the care of their parents under any circumstances. The government initiatives that are currently in place with a view to improving the circumstances of children in care are highlighted and the current thinking that underlies the practice of Guardians ad litem in their assessment of the best interests of the children they represent is explored. The chapter concludes with some reflections on the personal experiences of children for whom the state acts as parent.

Background

Public law proceedings are largely concerned with situations in which the state wishes to assume powers to make decisions about children which, normally, would be taken by their parents. These decisions involve matters such as where the child should live and with whom, whom they should see and how often, what schools they should attend and the nature of the arrangements that are made for their daily care.

Clearly extreme circumstances have to be shown to exist before the state would seek to interfere in family life, and it is the case that nearly all children who become subjects of public law proceedings have either been abandoned by their parents, are thought to have been ill-treated or otherwise inadequately cared for.

To obtain the court's authority to interfere in what would normally be considered private family business, the state must demonstrate that the child has, or is likely to, suffer significant harm, and that this is attributable to the care they receive from their parents. The state carries out these functions through social workers who are employed by local authorities. The Children Act 1989 provides the legislative context within which social work practice with children and families is conducted.

Which Children Come Before the Courts in Family Law Proceedings: Research Findings

The children and families who come to the attention of the child and family social work services, and ultimately the courts, are some of the most vulnerable and economically disadvantaged groups in our society. In a study of 2,500 children in thirteen local authorities, Bebbington and Miles (1989), found that only a quarter of children were living with both parents, almost three quarters of households were in receipt of income support and only one in five lived in owner-occupied housing. These researchers estimated the chances of two hypothetical children coming into care.

Child A and Child B, both aged between five and nine years. 'Child A' is white, lives in a two parent family with no dependence on social security, in an owner-occupied dwelling with more rooms than people, and two or less siblings. 'Child B' is of mixed race, lives in a privately rented home with one adult who is in receipt of income support, four or more other children, and where there is one or more persons per room. 'Child A' has a 1 in 7,000 chance of coming into care; Child B has a one in ten chance. This clearly demonstrates that those who have poorer access to resources are likely to be less able to give their children a good enough standard of parenting. As Coffield *et al.* (1981) so eloquently point out:

> ... *to miss the compelling force of external circumstances on the performance of the roles of a parent or child, and to imagine that a fragile household is not responsive to, and sometimes even torn apart by the pressures of poverty, unemployment and insecurity, is to attribute to poor people a freedom of choice and control over their lives which does not stand up to inquiry.*

Cleaver and Freeman (1995), identified five types of family to encompass the range of backgrounds of those children who were the subjects of investigations into suspected child abuse. They found that 43 per cent of the group they studied could be termed *multi-problem* families. This group was characterised by the length of time they had been known to the social services department and their wide-ranging and chronic difficulties. Parents in this group were likely to have themselves been abused in childhood.

A further 13 per cent of the sample were termed *acutely distressed* families. This group shared many of the characteristics of the *multi-problem* group, but they differed in respect of both the degree and frequency of the accidents and trauma they suffered.

A third group, comprising 21 per cent of the total sample and termed *specific problem* families, came to attention as a result of a particular suspicion, were not known to social services or similar agencies and were drawn from all social classes.

A further nine per cent were labelled *infiltrating perpetrators*, and covered those situations where known Schedule One offenders 'joined vulnerable, often single parent households. Schedule One' offenders are those who have been convicted of offences to children. The remaining 13 per cent were termed *outside perpetrators* and included those outside the family who abused or harmed children.

Other studies have consistently confirmed the findings of the Bebbington and Miles, and Cleaver and Freeman studies, and point to the economic and social disadvantages of the majority of the families who come to the attention of social services as a result of child care concerns (see for example Gibbons *et al.*, 1995; Parker and Farmer, 1991; and Wedge and Phelan, 1987). Parents who abuse or neglect their children are likely to have had poor experiences themselves in childhood which have ill equipped them for the demands of parenting. If the cycles of poverty and repeated family history are to be broken, it is important that effective intervention is provided to those who are known to be vulnerable, and as early as possible. This entails supporting parents to care for their children in order that these children do not themselves grow up with a history of disrupted attachments and insufficient good experiences to enable them to care for the next generation.

Much research which has focussed on the effectiveness of the child protection system suggests that children, and their families, are denied appropriate help at the initial stages of their contact with local authority child protection services, and thus it would seem, that a key aim of the Children Act 1989 has not been achieved (Department of Health, 1995). Where it is thought that a child is likely to have suffered, or is at risk of suffering harm, then the local authority has a duty to investigate the child's circumstances with a view to enabling it to decide what action to take (section 47, Children Act 1989). Prior to the introduction of the Children Act, the legislation only required the local authority to investigate whether the child's welfare required that other proceedings be instituted to enable the local authority to intervene in family life. The Children Act considerably widened the scope of the initial investigations into suspected child abuse with a view to ensuring that appropriate services could be provided in order to support parents in their care of their children. However, recent research as outlined below suggests that it has not been effective in meeting that objective.

Gibbons and her colleagues (1995), estimate that approximately 160,000 inquiries under section 47 take place each year in England. In around 25,000 of these investigations, suspicions of maltreatment or neglect are unsubstantiated. Research has shown that inquiries into suspicions of child abuse can have traumatic effects on families (Cleaver and Freeman, 1995), yet very often no assistance is provided after the investigations are completed. In more than half of the cases in Gibbons' study, the families investigated received no services, yet the families who were the subjects of the investigations were likely to have been multiply disadvantaged. Assessments tended to be focussed on whether or not abuse had taken place as opposed to a comprehensive examination of the child's needs. Appropriate help was not always offered as a result of the assessments that were undertaken. In a series of studies commissioned by the Department of Health, in 1995, the general consensus of opinion is that too high a percentage of available resources is directed towards assessment. In the report, *Responding to Families in Need: The Inspection of Assessment, Planning and Decision Making in Family Support Services* (1997), it was found that, whilst too many children were the subjects of unnecessary investigations, others slipped through the child protection net and were left in conditions of neglect for too long.

This emphasis on supporting family life is based on findings from a great number of studies which are consistent in pointing to the benefits that family ties bestow on children. Children brought up by their families generally do better than those cared for by the state in a number of important respects such as health (physical and emotional), education, employment, housing, income etc (Jackson (1987); The Utting Report (1991); Department of Health and OFSTED (1995); Bamford and Wolkind (1988); and Stein (1989)). These studies show that when children are cared for by the state, responsibility for ensuring routine dental treatment, immunisations, health checks, and school and career planning, falls between foster carers, social workers and parents, with the result that many children do not have these routine needs met. Children who move around in care are more vulnerable than those in long-term placements, and it is these children who are at greatest risk of not having the same kind of attention paid to routine dental and medical care as children who receive consistent parenting.

Children who move around in care are also vulnerable to long term emotional damage as a result of not being provided with the opportunity to form secure attachments with adults whom they can depend upon to provide consistent, good quality care in a context of warmth and acceptance. Figures provided by the Department of Health (1999), for the years 1996/7, suggest that about one in every six children admitted to local authority care during the course of a year have more than one admission to care (these figures exclude that group of children who have a series of planned short admissions to care), and that some 390 children had five or more admissions during the course of a year. It is not uncommon for up to 40 per cent of children admitted to care to have had previous admissions and, in some authorities the figures are much higher, for example 53 per cent in one local authority. It is unlikely that those children who have repeated, unplanned admissions to care will be able to return to those who cared for them on previous occasions.

When children are admitted to care they are likely to experience several changes of placement. Statistics provided by the Department of Health (1999), at the end of March 1998 suggest that 39 per cent of children will be moved during their first month in care. After six months in care, the figures fall to around 10–12 per cent of children who undergo a change of placement. There is wide geographical variation; the better local authorities achieve rates of five per cent of looked after children changing placement within three months, whilst those who perform least well have unacceptably high rates of 25 per cent.

The statistics further show that, on average, only about 50 per cent of children who have been in care for four years or more had placements that had lasted for at least two years, or had been placed for adoption. Again there is wide variation depending on the local authority area in which the child lives. Some achieve long term placement for 90–100 per cent of children in their care; others manage to provide stability for less than 20 per cent of children. Of the 94,000 placements made during the year ending 31 March 1997, approximately a quarter lasted less than eight days. These figures point to chronic instability as a feature of life for many looked after children, and also suggest that some authorities have better developed services than others.

In the Department of Health's *Modernising Health and Social Services, National Priorities Guidance* (1999), the government set a target for local authorities to reduce to 'no more than 16 per cent of looked-after children those who have three or more placement changes within one year', in the hope of making the performance of the top 25 per cent of local authorities standard practice nationally. Improvements in adoption services are also a key aim of the government's *Quality Protects* programme. Two recent reports, *For Children's Sake: An SSI Inspection of Local Authority Adoption Services* (1996), and *Part II An Inspection of Local Authority Post-Placement and Post-Adoption Services* (1997), both found that adoption was often an unnecessarily lengthy process. The average time children spend in local authority care prior to their adoption is in the region of three and a half years. This is a long time for children to be 'in limbo', with no sense of adult people being responsible for their permanent care.

It is clear that, despite the intention of parliament in the drafting of the Children Act 1989, appropriate support is not always made available to children and their families at a sufficiently early stage. In fact, the system is experienced by children and their parents as punitive and traumatic (Cleaver and Freeman, 1995) as a result of the emphasis on proving abuse, with much less attention paid to identifying the needs of children, and putting in resources to address the difficulties. Improved and more efficient assessment of the needs of children and families are seen as the key to providing better targeted support delivered more efficiently.

Government Initiatives

The Department of Health, in March 2000, launched the *Framework for Assessment of Children in Need and their Families*. This provides for initial assessments, where it is thought that a child may be suffering harm, to be completed within seven days and followed by core assessments within 35 days. The assessments must take account of the child's developmental needs, the capacity of the parents to respond to these needs, and relevant wider family and environmental factors. The use of evidence to justify the judgements that are made about children's needs is emphasised. The aim is to ensure that children and families receive a comprehensive assessment of their needs, and the help they require, at an early stage. For the first time a performance standard in terms of speed of response is linked with assessment and provision of services. Also, the ratio of expenditure between family support and children looked after is now recognised as a measure of the extent to which family support is being prioritised, and this is included as a performance indicator in the assessment of local authorities' performance within the *Quality Protects* programme

In response to the continuing concerns about the effectiveness of the child care system, repeatedly raised by researchers, the government introduced the *Quality Protects* programme in September 1998. Eight comprehensive and outcome-focussed objectives for the improvement of services to children were set. The eight identified objectives are to ensure that:

- Children are securely attached to carers capable of providing safe and effective care for the duration of their childhood.
- Children are protected from emotional, physical, or sexual abuse and neglect (significant harm).
- Children gain maximum life chance benefits from educational opportunities, health care and social care.
- Young people leaving care, as they enter adulthood, are not isolated and participate socially and economically as citizens.
- Children with specific social needs arising out of disability or a health condition are living in families or other appropriate settings in the community where their assessed needs are adequately met and reviewed.
- Referral and assessment processes discriminate effectively between different types and levels of need and produce a timely service response.
- Resources are planned and provided at levels which represent best value for money, allow for choice and for different responses for different needs and circumstances.

The *Quality Protects* programme lasts for three years and funds have been set aside which local authorities can access if they can demonstrate how the manner in which they wish to spend it will lead to the objectives being met. Performance indicators by which the impact on the services to children and families can be measured were identified, and systems have been set up to monitor the performance of local authorities in achieving the set objectives. For the first time, children's ability to offer constructive comment on their experience of the services they receive is acknowledged. Their participation is actively promoted through a special grant being made available to local authorities to assist them in involving children in the development of services and policy, and, in turn, local authorities are required to show that children's views are reflected in the planning, monitoring and evaluation of children's services.

Assistance with the development of practical parenting skills, often through group work at family centres, together with the provision of counselling, emotional and practical support, and the skills of the child and family psychiatric services, are all used by local authorities to support parents in the care of their children. Section 17 of the Children Act 1989 lays a duty upon local authorities to provide certain services, and a permissive power to provide others.

In March 1999, the Social Services Inspectorate published its report, *Getting Family Support Right*, which presented the findings of a study into the delivery of family support services within eight local authorities. Attempts were made to identify best practice and provide guidance for managers of family support services with the aim of ensuring that families are offered appropriate and effective support. Good practice dictates that such services should be provided within a time scale that is appropriate to the needs of the child in question, and this will depend on their age and previous experience. Children cannot be expected to wait indefinitely in the hope that their situation will improve.

The impact of support and assistance provided to parents needs to be monitored and assessed within a clearly identified timeframe. It should only be when all reasonable efforts have failed that local authorities should seek, through the courts, permission to intervene in family life. The courts expect, and the legislation requires, that all reasonable efforts have been made to assist parents in their care of their children with a view to avoiding the need to bring proceedings. The local authority will of course have to explain to the court its intentions in respect of the care it would provide for the child. Such information is usually set out in a document called 'the care plan'. Prior to bringing the matter before the court, it would be appropriate for the local authority to explore whether members of the child's wider extended family could care for them.

Children in the care of the state often miss out on the process of planning for the future, a process that goes on in most families over several years, in which children's strengths are identified and acknowledged, their development is encouraged, and related to possible career and employment paths, sometimes guided by discussions with teachers at parent teacher consultation evenings. Perhaps the most important aspect of a child's future opportunities is their educational attainment. Children in the care of the state fare much less well than those who grow up in their own families in terms of educational attainment. The Department of Health estimates that, in the worst local authorities, as few as 25 per cent of such children leave school with GCSE or GNVQ qualifications as compared to the national rate of 93 per cent.

The Social Exclusion Unit report, *Truancy and Social Exclusion* (1998), states that the permanent exclusion rate for children in the care of the state is ten times higher than the national average and suggests that as many as 30 per cent of children in care are either excluded from school or fail to attend. Educational attainment rates appear to deteriorate as children get older but even at age seven, evidence from a pilot study conducted in three local authorities during 1997/98 points to children in care of the state doing significantly less well than their peers. This is yet another area which *Quality Protects* is intended to address and which had been identified as a 'National Priority'.

Targets for local authorities have been set which require that, by 2001, at least 50 per cent of children looked after by them will leave school with GCSE or GNVQ equivalent, and this figure is intended to rise to 75 per cent by 2003. Measures in place are improved data collection systems to enable local authorities to be aware, and to monitor the progress, of children in their care. In addition councillors are to be given regular reports in order that they may be encouraged to take an active interest in the resources that are made available to assist children with their educational development. Under the *Quality Protects* initiative, local authorities are required to produce annual statistics on all children in care, though there has been insufficient time, and information has not yet been made available, upon which to judge the success of the programme.

It is the case that the Looked after Children (LAC) record forms were expected to address this by focusing attention on all of these issues and on the specific health and educational needs of each child at six monthly reviews. However the evidence (see *Someone Else's Children. Responding to Families in Need: The Inspections of Assessment, Planning and Decision Making in Family Support Services For Children Looked After and the Safety of Children Looked After* (DoH, 1998), suggests that such forms are not always completed fully. In any event they do not in themselves allow for the local authority managers and councillors to have an overview of all children in care in their areas, and the extent to which health and educational needs are met generally.

The *Looked After Children* system, which is designed to ensure regular monitoring and review of the well-being of looked after children, is being further developed and will be linked with the *Framework for Assessment* procedures introduced in 2000, as well as with other current initiatives such as the *Quality Protects* programme. The intention is to provide a more systematic and coherent structure within which plans that safeguard the welfare of children in care can be designed and reviewed. Seven dimensions have been identified which form the basis upon which the six monthly reviews of looked after children should be conducted. They are:

1. How well children are doing in their education.
2. Their health.
3. Their emotional and behavioral development.
4. Their sense of identity and self-esteem.
5. Their relationships with their family and friends.
6. How well they fit in socially.
7. Whether they are acquiring the practical skills they need to look after themselves.

The Children Act 1989 is based on principles of good practice in the care of the child which have been largely derived from research. The *Quality Protects* initiative, the *Framework for Assessment procedures* (2000) and the *National Priorities Guidance* (1999) all represent the mechanisms by which it is hoped that current practice can be improved and developed and, together, they paint a picture of the current issues with which social work practitioners are grappling. Social work with children and families is a constantly changing picture. It may be better tomorrow, and we hope that it will be, but it is important to acknowledge that a great many children are living with the system, and all its many imperfections, at present.

The Child's Experience of Being Cared for by the State

It is important here to explore, from the child's perspective, some of the ways in which the system fails those who are cared for by the state. When a child cannot be cared for by their parents they, typically, will blame themselves at least to some extent, and many experience a sense of having been rejected by their parents because they were not good enough. Even infants who have been adopted at birth, and have never known their parents, report in adult life feelings of personal failure, of not being good enough, of being unworthy of love.

Children who have had an unhappy experience of family life which eventually leads to them being excluded from their families, are even more vulnerable to feelings of low self esteem. Many will have had the experience of their parent putting alcohol, drugs, sexual fulfillment, dangerous partners or dangerous lifestyles before the child themselves. Others will have experienced the brunt of a parent's temper in the form of excessive physical punishment and see this as evidence on which to base their fear that, had they themselves been somehow different, then their parents may have been able to love them. When one considers the emotional experience of those children whose circumstances are so extreme that the authorities wish to intervene in their lives, it is hardly surprising that many have problems when cared for by the state.

For children who feel unworthy of their parents' love, it is easy to believe that foster carers, and residential social workers who care for them, are motivated by financial gain or some other ulterior motive. When children believe that it is someone's job to care for them they can deny the human element of their relations with others, and thus they have little reason to make any personal investment in the relationship. If they have no reason to please or not to upset those who care for them, it is easy to justify behaviour which is sometimes bad, more often self centered. Arguments and disputes become difficult to resolve in the absence of personal investment in relationships and thus, relations can easily break down irretrievably, resulting in children having to move from one carer to another, or one children's home to another. With each successive move the damage to the child's self-esteem is greater. It is not difficult to see how children in such situations are unable to get the best of what is on offer in the educational system.

Poor self-esteem and other negative personal feelings act to prevent children feeling positive about their achievements. They are often further hampered by feelings about being different from their peers, and embarrassment about having to explain their circumstances to curious children who have not come across foster carers, or who cannot grasp why anyone of their age would not be looked after by a parent. My own children's experience in school provides a graphic illustration of this. Prior to a child who had recently entered the care system joining their class, the school headmistress spoke with the children about how 'little Johnny' was not lucky, like themselves, in that he didn't have a nice mummy or daddy to look after him. She asked the class of seven year olds to be patient with this child who, she feared, might be very naughty. Judging by the children's discussions, later overheard at home, one can only imagine the things that were put to this little boy in the playground!

In addition the system does not make it easy for children, who are cared for by the state, to relate on equal terms with their peers. When little Johnny's residential social workers tried to ease him into local life, they invited some of his class mates to tea. The staff did, however, have to telephone the parents of these children and ask for a financial contribution to the cost of the meal in line with county policy! Also, when Johnny was invited to a 'sleep over', permission could only be granted after the event was long over, because of the need to undertake police checks in accordance with the regulations governing children in care (The Children Act 1989, Guidance and Regulations, Volume 4).

Conclusion

Social work practice with children and families should be based on supporting families to care for their children wherever possible. Guardians are conscious that all the evidence points, in most cases, to families being better able to do this than the state. For a small number of children, and figures for previous years suggest that this group is increasing in number (Department of Health, 1999), it is not conducive to their welfare to remain with their families. The key issues facing practitioners are the need to develop preventative practice, to devote time and resources to assist families at an early stage in their contact with the authorities and, when this has failed, to provide a better service for those children who rely on the state for their parenting. Children's guardians will be influenced by the extent to which efforts to help the child remain with its family have been properly and fully explored when carrying out the delicate task of balancing the advantages and disadvantages of the care system for a particular child. In critically appraising the work of the local authorites concerned they will have regard to the extent to which current government initiatives aimed at improving practice within child care have found expression in policy, procedures and practice.

3 The Role of the Guardian ad litem: A Personal View

Maria Ruegger

Introduction

The role of the Guardian ad litem generally is set out in detail in *The Manual of Practice Guidance for Guardians ad litem* (Department of Health, 1992). The focus in this chapter is upon the way in which Guardians involved in family proceedings carry out their tasks on behalf of children and the courts. It is intended that this very personal account, which is not necessarily representative of all Guardian ad litem practice, will be of interest to other Guardians who may wish to compare and contrast their own particular style with that described. It is also intended that it will be of interest to those readers who are joining CAFCASS from different professional groups who may wish to know more of the mechanics of the Guardian's job, and to those who currently work closely with Guardians but are not familiar with the full scope of their professional activities.

As a Guardian ad litem, I see my primary task as keeping the focus of all the parties and the court on the needs and interests of the child throughout the proceedings. I am usually appointed very soon after the local authority notifies the court of its intention to apply for an order in respect of a particular child. The first thing I do is to speak with the child's social worker on the telephone. I will, of course, have been given copies of the application and any evidence filed in support of it, such as the social worker's first statement, and perhaps medical, psychological, educational and police reports, although it is rarely the case that one has a complete set of available information at the outset of proceedings.

The information I seek from the social worker at the first point of contact is about more than the facts of the case. It is concerned with:

- How the child and the adults are feeling about matters and each other.
- The extent to which alternatives have been explored, for example whether any members of the wider family network are able to offer alternatives to care both during the proceedings and afterwards.
- What has been done with a view to avoiding the need to take proceedings.

The Guardian's Role Prior to, and at, the First Hearing for Directions

The appointment of expert witnesses

Sometimes it is the case that everything possible has been offered to assist parents to care for their child, and that all alternatives have been fully explored, for example the assistance that might be offered by relatives.

At other times one finds that the assessment of the ability to parent has not been fully explored. This might be to do with the fact that the child protection system tends to focus on detection of failure, at the expense of offering support to families in need at an early stage. For example, this can arise where parents who have a learning disability have not been offered the kind of support appropriate to their particular needs which might have resulted in them being able to develop their parenting capacities. Appropriate expertise may not be brought in until care proceedings have already been initiated, rather than when problems were still being identified, when parents may have been more amenable to help offered via the local authority.

Sometimes an assessment is not complete because the child has only very recently come to the attention of social services, and the circumstances were such that immediate legal intervention was considered necessary, for example, in the case of suspected non-accidental injury. In those cases where a full assessment of the parents' capacity to provide a good standard of care for their children is not available, I will discuss with the child's solicitor, the social worker, the parents and their legal representatives, the form that such an assessment might take, the likely time-scale involved and whether expert or residential assessments are desirable. I might also raise, at this stage, the question of whether any expertise is required in order further to understand the child's particular needs. For example, if it is proposed to move a child from carers to whom he has become attached (and who wish to offer him a permanent home), but who do not reflect his racial and cultural heritage, then I would be likely to consider that the court would benefit from having expert advice on the relative importance of attachment and identity for that particular child.

In certain situations it is essential to have an expert opinion, as the relevant matters are not within the expertise of Guardians; for example, where there is a question of whether a child has been subjected to sexual abuse, or the significance of diagnostic tests when non-accidental injury is suspected. The various parties and I may have different views about what is necessary, but it is helpful nonetheless if these can be identified and recorded at an early stage, if possible, before the first court hearing. This is because it is the court which will decide whether any such assessments would assist it in reaching a final decision on the matters before it, and if so, who should carry out such an assessment. I would also seek to inform the child about any proposals for experts, and to explore with the child their feelings about this, in order that such information can be conveyed to the court.

The Guardian has a particular duty to assist the court in the management of the case and to that end should play an active and enquiring role in the matter of the appointment of expert witnesses. Sometimes I find myself opposing such requests by other parties. Unless there is a clear area of expertise which is not already available within the knowledge bases of the social worker, other local authority witnesses and the Guardian, then I take the view that it is not in the child's interest to appoint experts. My reasons are to do with avoiding unnecessary delay (which it is acknowledged can be harmful to children), the unfairness of exposing children to unnecessary forensic investigations from which they are unlikely to benefit, and because the appointment of experts (who simply duplicate the work of others), is a strain on the public purse.

The appointment of experts, generally, introduces an element of delay into the proceedings, which can be considerable. Few expert reports are available in less than three months and although the initial instruction is usually joint, one of the parties may return to court to ask for leave to obtain a second opinion from a different expert if the initial recommendation is not to their liking. When experts recommend further assessment then more time will elapse while the arrangements are set up, the assessment takes place (which may last weeks or even months), reports are written and parties have the opportunity to reflect and comment on them. Not only may the resulting delay be inherently harmful to children, it may in effect reduce the options open to the court by the time of the Final Hearing as the family dynamics change and the attachments children have formed with their carers in the interim must be taken into account in determining their best interests. For example, I recently learnt of a case that lasted two years as a result of expert involvement, by which time the baby was two years old and had only known one set of carers. The issue for determination by the court was whether there should be an attempt at rehabilitation. The Guardian and the local authority were opposed to this on the basis that the court had already made findings, after hearing detailed evidence, in respect of the parents being responsible for a number of serious injuries inflicted upon the children, allegations which they continued to deny. A psychiatrist who specialised in work with adults, was appointed by the parents, but had recommended that the parents be offered a residential assessment prior to the Final Hearing. Rather than proceeding to a hearing on this recommendation at that stage, a decision was taken to seek a second opinion. The second expert required a lengthy period of assessment before concluding that further assessment would be desirable. The judge refused to direct this and insisted that the Final Hearing should proceed forthwith. As it is for the judge, rather than the expert, to make the final decision, then with the benefit of hindsight it was clear that the obtaining of further expert opinion would not materially assist and therefore would lead only to unnecessary delay of several months in making permanent decisions for these children's futures. Also, these children were cared for by persons about whom there were some concerns, but insufficient to warrant removing them given the strength of their attachments after two years. Had matters proceeded to a Final Hearing earlier it is likely that some very different arrangements would have been made for these children's care.

This example is not intended to suggest that second opinions should never be obtained. It is of course the case that experts do at times disagree with one another, and that it is often only with the benefit of hindsight that one can assess the value of their respective contributions. It is also the case that the court must consider human rights issues when deciding whether to allow the appointment of further experts, if the recommendation of the first is not to the liking of one or more of the parties. In forming my own view on requests by any party to instruct further expert opinion I endeavour to explore whether, and in what way, the expertise already obtained is thought to be inadequate.

Where experts are to be appointed it is essential that it is clear that what they have to contribute will also assist the court in determining the particular issues in respect of the child with whom it is concerned. Often I have queried the purpose of obtaining detailed educational psychological assessments in the course of proceedings. This is not to suggest that I think such assessments are of no value to children when making decisions about their education. I simply question whether the detail of IQ testing is of value to the court and whether it would not, in many cases, be sufficient for the court to know that such assessments are being made alongside the court proceedings in order to enable the local authority to make proper plans for the child's education. These concerns are based partly on the undesirability of exposing children to assessments, the details of which are made known to many who are not directly involved in planning for their education and partly on the escalating delay and expense that obtaining and commenting on such reports involves. Of course, sometimes detailed educational psycho-logical assessments are certainly warranted. However, the onus should be on the parties to satisfy the court that, in addition to being useful the assessment will materially advance the child's interests in the court proceedings.

Sometimes there is no disagreement about the nature of the child's needs, but the necessary resources are not being made available to them. By commissioning expert reports on how a child's needs can best be met, the Guardian can invite the court to exert pressure on those responsible for the allocation of resources. The process by which this occurs is that the Guardian requests the judge to direct that the person responsible for deciding upon the allocation of resources should attend court in person to explain how it is proposed that the child's needs be met in the light of the agreed expert opinion. Experience suggests that pressure of this sort can often produce hitherto unavailable resources. Whilst reports obtained for this purpose could not be said to be necessary to assist the court in the discharge of the case, they do enable the Guardian, through the court, to take into account the long term needs of children.

The Guardian has a particular duty to assist the court in the management of the case and, to that end, should play an active and enquiring role in the matter of the appointment of expert witnesses. Whilst their judicious appointment can be of great help in particular cases, the Guardian must ensure that the potential benefit to the child outweighs the possible harm to him through the inevitable delay and, where it is necessary, the need for the child to see yet another professional.

The appointment of a solicitor for the child

In advance of the First Hearing, I appoint a solicitor from the Children Panel to represent the child. In deciding whom to instruct, I try to ensure that I obtain the best possible legal representation for the child concerned, so I will not instruct those of whom I do not have personal experience nor, alternatively, those who do not come highly recommended by colleagues. There has been much disquiet expressed by solicitors who have been recently appointed to the Children Panel about the fact that they find it hard to obtain instructions from Guardians, and some suggestions for the adoption of systems that would ensure that work is equally distributed. I take the view however that, by acting for parents, such solicitors will soon become known by Guardians, and those Guardians in turn tell other Guardians about those whom they would themselves instruct on behalf of children. The Guardian ad litem and the solicitor work closely together. I have found that having a solicitor with the right qualities, makes a significant difference to the way in which cases progress. In addition to having well developed advocacy skills, and the ability to work co-operatively with their colleagues, a solicitor needs to relate easily to children, many of whom are unhappy and exhibit varying degrees of disturbed behaviour.

The solicitor will not normally see the child before the First Hearing unless it is thought that the child may be old enough to give their own instructions, a subject that is dealt with by Sarah Stevens in Chapter 6. As a Guardian I would usually discuss with the solicitor, in advance of the First Hearing, the kind of directions, or preliminary discussions that I think may be helpful, and the time-scale within which we aim to operate. If I feel an expert would be advisable I, or the solicitor, will try to identify one able to report within a reasonable time to minimise delay.

Seeing the child

My next job will be to see the child, usually wherever they are living. On my first meeting with children I give them a specially designed calendar to keep, on which I mark important dates, such as future appointments and court hearings. I explain to all children who are old enough to understand (and most five year olds fall into this category), that the most important part of my job is to find out what they think about what has happened already, what they would like to happen in the future, and anything else they consider to be important, so that I can tell the judge their views. I explain that I have to write a report and that they might want to help me write the part that is about their wishes, or at least check it out to make sure I get it right. I explain the role of legal representatives generally, and tell the child about their own solicitor.

I tell children that another part of my job is to talk to people who know them, in order to find out what they think should happen, after which I make up my own mind about what I think is best. I take trouble to ensure that the child understands that whilst this is sometimes the same as what they want for themselves, sometimes it is not, in which case I will tell them. I explain to children that I used to be a social worker but that now I work just for the courts, and I try to get across to them in meaningful ways the concept of independence from the local authority, the differences between myself and their social workers. I also give similar information to parents about the nature of the Guardian's roles, both in writing and verbally, during my first interview with them.

A number of studies have shown that very young children can give a clear account of matters within their personal experience if they are interviewed appropriately (Davies *et al.*, 1986; Dent and Flin, 1992; Vizard, 1991). These studies demonstrate that ability is dependent not simply on age but arises from a complex interaction of factors such as the importance the child attaches to the topic of discussion, their linguistic fluency and how they are questioned. These studies contain useful guidance for those whose work requires them to engage with children and to ascertain their wishes and feelings.

One of the difficult tasks in interviewing children is to balance the need to give them full information against overloading them. My decision as to whether to explain the intricacies of separate representation at this first meeting is based on whether I think that child can reasonably take in this detail, at this point, and this will be affected by their age, level of understanding and concentration, and the extent to which I judge them to be engaged and interested. For a more detailed discussion on this subject the reader should refer to Priscilla Alderson's account of her research on children who require surgery (Alderson, 1993).

I also explain to children at the first interview the differences between civil and criminal proceedings, and attempt to dispel any fears or fantasies they may have from watching 'The Bill' and similar programmes. I tell them about the process of court hearings, and particularly about how the judge listens carefully to everyone before deciding what should happen. I will also raise the question of expert witnesses, if this is likely to be relevant to the particular child, and tell them about their right to give or withhold consent to medical examination and assessments that are for forensic purposes if they are of sufficient understanding to make an informed decision. I finish by explaining what is likely to happen as far as I know this myself, arranging future appointments which, together, we note on the calendar, and by ensuring that the child knows that our work together finishes after the court proceedings come to an end. The calendar that I give to children contains information about much of what we spoke of, and gives contact numbers for myself and the child's solicitor. Much of this content is re-visited during future meetings, particularly the idea that my role ends with the completion of the Final Hearing.

When children are pre-verbal, have limited understanding or have difficulty in expressing themselves, I try to ascertain their wishes by communicating with them through play. With older children I might use drawing and sentence completion materials as a means of helping them to talk about their wishes and feelings. I meet with children on a number of occasions and in a range of different settings. This always includes their homes, and might also include their nursery school or play group, as well the family centre where appropriate. If possible I will see children with each of their parents separately and sometimes, also, with others who are well known to them. I will also make efforts to see them at different times of their day, such as meal times and bed times, particularly if I am considering rehabilitation with parents, or placement with members of the extended family.

Interviewing parents
My next task is to see parents. I explain to them my role and also give them written information that they can refer to later. I explain how I intend to proceed with my assessment, whom I plan to see, how often I will see the children and where, and the nature of the other tasks I intend to carry out, for example, reading local authority files on themselves and sometimes, also, other relevant files. On some occasions I might wish to speak with their doctors and I would seek their permission to do so, having explained why I think this is an appropriate course of action. If experts' assessments are on the agenda then I would seek to explain to parents why I think such assessments would be helpful. I try to ensure that parents understand that part of my task is to appraise the work of the local authority and that I am independent from social services. I also give parents an opportunity to suggest to me anyone else whom I should see or attempt to contact. It is important that parents experience the Guardian as being independent, particularly so in relation to the local authority. The reader may wish to refer to a detailed account of working with parents in public law proceedings (Ruegger, 1999), and to a moving account of a parent's experience of his involvement in such proceedings (Tosey, 1999), for further discussion on this important, and often overlooked, subject.

Case management and planning
For the First Hearing, I invariably prepare an interim report, the purpose being to ensure that the focus of all involved is on the needs of the child in respect of the management and time-tabling of the case, and of the arrangements for the child pending the Final Hearing. In so doing, I aim to avoid delay by identifying at an early stage what I think needs to be done, and by whom, in order that any disagreements on these issues can be resolved sooner rather than later.

At the First Hearing for directions the aim should, if possible, be to timetable the case to the Final Hearing. This involves setting down dates for the filing of evidence and reports. Typically the parents will file their statements and any evidence upon which they wish to rely, followed by the local authority and then, where relevant, the expert witnesses. Both parents and the local authority will have an opportunity to file further statements, commenting on the material filed to date, and the local authority will, in addition, be required to file its Care Plan. The Guardian ad litem is always the last to submit their report as they are required to comment on all the evidence filed. Clearly, if parties do not adhere to the timetable from the outset then slippage is likely to get gradually worse as the case progresses. If the dates for the Final Hearing are to be retained then the Guardian will need to keep an eye on the filing of evidence as and when it becomes due and, if it is late, then enquiries need to be made. If it appears to the Guardian that the Final Hearing dates are likely to be jeopardised by the late filing of evidence then they should bring the matter to the court's attention at an early stage so that appropriate steps can be taken.

   If it is not possible to timetable the case at the First Hearing for directions, then it is important to ensure an early return to court for a Hearing for further directions, in order that delay in achieving a final resolution is avoided.

The Guardian's Investigation

The Guardian's investigation in general
Throughout the course of the proceedings I always aim to be clear about the purpose of any inquiries I make, or interviews I conduct, both with children and with adults. The Guardian must gather information upon which to form a view as to the likely best interests of the child and will do so within the framework detailed in the first part of this chapter. They must also keep the children informed about the progress of the proceedings as well as ascertain their wishes and feelings about the decision the court must make. Guardians usually see children on a number of different occasions and, where possible, in different settings. Typically, the Guardian's assessment will involve seeing children alone, with their sibling groups, with their parents and, where appropriate, with their carers.

   In addition to their direct work with children, Guardians also interview parents and other significant adults in the child's life. They are also likely to consult with the child's health visitor, teacher, social worker and other relevant professionals, to help in reaching a view as to the child's best interests.

   Guardians are expected to keep detailed records of their investigations and may be asked for them in court.

Working with expert witnesses
Where expert reports have been ordered by the court, the Guardian, given their independent role in the proceedings, will often be invited to take the lead. The professional, as opposed to administrative, tasks involved in this process include drafting a letter of instruction for each expert, and liaising with other parties to agree the questions that need to be put to the experts.

This can be a complex task; parents' advocates sometimes wish to have questions phrased in such a way as to ensure that negative comments about their clients are discouraged, and Guardians and social workers may phrase questions according to the answers they expect or would like. Whether or not the Guardian is given the lead in the instruction of the experts it is, in my view, most important that they take a very active role in ensuring that the questions posed to the experts will elicit answers which will best assist the court. The kinds of questions the experts are asked can have a very significant impact on the quality of the assessment they produce. It is my experience that the drafting, circulating and re-drafting process is unlikely to be completed in less than a period of three weeks.

If agreements between the parties are difficult to obtain then it is important that the Guardian consider whether they should refer the matter back to court. Experts cannot begin work without the letter of instruction and, as they take longer than anyone else to complete their enquiries, because of their relatively late appointment in the proceedings combined with their other clinical commitments, it is easy to understand how delay in agreeing letters of instruction can seriously prejudice the court timetable. A brief Hearing for directions can be extremely helpful in concentrating the minds of those concerned, and agreements are reached much more quickly at the court room door than they are through the exchange of numerous faxes between offices.

If a number of experts have reported then it is usual for the court to require the Guardian, or the Guardian's solicitor, to convene an experts meeting in which matters of agreement, and those which are in dispute, can be identified. At such a meeting the Guardian should ensure that detailed minutes are taken and circulated to each expert, with a request that they suggest amendments, or agree them as accurate by signing and returning. This avoids any misunderstanding and ensures that the Guardian is protected should experts change their views between the meeting and the Final Hearing. If some experts are unable to attend the meeting then it is also advisable to circulate them with copies of the questions posed to their colleagues, together with their answers, with a view to seeking to incorporate all relevant views into a statement dealing with matters in agreement and dispute. This process can save a great deal of time at the final hearing as live evidence can be restricted to those matters which are not agreed between the experts. Mr Justice Wall has issued guidelines (*Re CB and JB Care Proceedings: Guidelines* [1998] 2 FLR) that are helpful to practitioners who are charged with responsibility for clarifying matters of agreement and dispute between experts.

Examining the case records
Another task that the Guardian undertakes at an early stage in the proceedings involves examining the social work records. In doing so, particular care needs to be taken to separate fact from opinion, and as Timms (1992) helpfully points out, the identification 'of circumstances in

which hearsay evidence has been allowed to acquire the status of truth through frequent repetition' is something one has to look out for. Whilst it is not normally necessary to read every single diary entry, it is important to see all the sequential records relating to case conferences, reviews, referral sheets and communications from third parties, such as medical or educational reports. Section 42 of the Children Act 1989 authorises Guardians to take copies of relevant information from local authority files, to refer in their report to documents seen and, if necessary, to produce them in court. The Guardian, like other parties, can also seek orders from the court to have other professional records released when necessary, for example medical records and police records and statements.

Intervening on behalf of children during the currency of proceedings
As the case progresses the Guardian should be kept informed and consulted about matters to do with the child, such as change of placement, or alterations to arrangements for contact. If the Guardian is unhappy about issues relevant to the welfare of the child, or the progress of the case, then she can refer the matter back to court for directions. For example, a Guardian colleague recently described to me how three children for whom she was appointed had expressed their despair and distress at being separated from each other in their foster care placements, and about their lack of opportunity to visit their parents and each other. When the Guardian's attempts to persuade the local authority to find a more suitable placement for all three children failed, the Guardian gave notice to the court, and the other parties, that she intended to oppose the making of further interim care orders and to seek an interim contact order under section 8 of the Children Act 1989. As both parents were in prison and there was no other suitable carer, it is difficult to see how any opposition to the renewal of interim care orders could have been successful. However, the Guardian's intention was to put pressure on the local authority through rehearsing arguments about the children's current needs, wishes and feelings before the court and this strategy was indeed successful as a suitable placement, together with the finance to secure it, was found. Arrangements were also made to enable the children to visit their parents in prison.

Perhaps more common are children's expressions of distress about contact arrangements. Again, if negotiations fail, Guardians will consider making an application for an interim contact order on behalf of the children. Some cases will involve parents or other parties contesting the making or renewal of interim care orders. There are a wide range of other applications which may be made. For example, the police might apply for disclosure of papers from the care proceedings to use within criminal proceedings, persons may apply for party status, DNA testing may be sought with a view to establishing paternity, or someone may be seeking a residential assessment of the parent's capacity to provide care. In each case the Guardian must consider the order sought from the point of view of the child. The structure within which I undertake this task is that provided by the welfare checklist (section 3, Children Act 1989). It is almost always the case that the Guardian will prepare interim reports when interim care orders are contested and likely that they will produce a written report on other matters requiring the court's determination prior to the Final Hearing. Usually the headings set out in section 1 (3) (a) of the Children Act 1989 provide the format for such reports.

The Guardian's Report and the Final Hearing

When investigations are complete, and I am writing my report, I involve the child in deciding which of the things they have told me, go into the section of my final report dealing with their wishes and feelings. I might also assist the child to think through the implications that this written evidence may have for their future relations with family members. It is at this stage that I raise with some children the question of whether they wish to attend court, whilst making it clear to them that the final decision on this lies with the judge. If I consider that it would not be in a particular child's interests to attend court then I would not raise the possibility. I take the view that very young children would either be overwhelmed by the formality of the occasion or very bored by the proceedings. Older children who exhibit disturbed behaviour are likely to be ejected from proceedings if they misbehave, and this is not likely to benefit them. Sometimes it is possible to bring children to court at a time when the court is not in session so that they can see the building. This can, in my experience, assist children in feeling more involved and informed, whilst protecting them from the pressure of having to sit quietly whilst everyone else discusses their previous and future lives, the shortcomings of their parents and sometimes even their own shortcomings.

The Guardian plays a key role in the Final Hearing. They are in court throughout the proceedings and assist the solicitor for the child by advising on matters to be put to witnesses, both lay and professional. The Guardian has the privileged position of being the last witness to be called and being the last party to cross examine the witnesses of other parties. This enables them to 'sweep up', so that any matters which have not been fully dealt with, or which later evidence has sought to contradict, can properly be put before the court. In giving evidence last, the Guardian, together with the child's solicitor, can decide which are the most important matters to focus on from the child's perspective.

If the outcome is not in accordance with the Guardian's recommendation then they, together with the child's solicitor, must consider whether to issue notice of appeal.

Tying Up Loose Ends

Where expert witnesses have been involved directly with children I try to ensure that they are aware of the outcome of the proceedings. I always ask the child from whom they would like to learn the final decision of the court, and try to ensure that this happens. Whether or not this person is myself, I arrange to see children following the end of the proceedings in order to say good-bye and, where appropriate, ensure that they know how to contact their solicitor in the future. My final task, before closing the case, is to write a letter to the child that is either placed on their file or given to their carers so that, in years to come, if they wish to try to understand the reasons behind the important decisions affecting their future that were made in their childhood, an explanation will be available. For a detailed discussion of this aspect of guardian practice see Gillian Norris's account in Chapter 5.

Conclusion

The role of the Guardian is time-limited and focussed. It ends when the proceedings, and any appeal, are complete. From the outset, it is the Guardian's task to raise the profile of the child at every stage and when any decision has to be made. The Guardian must also act as the mouthpiece for the child and, in combining these two roles, must tread a careful path between rights and best interests. It would not be appropriate here to analyse the extent to which the rights and welfare models influence Guardian practice. This is not something which can usefully be done by examining the practice of one individual, rather it is a matter that is best left to the kind of detailed study yet to be undertaken by researchers.

4 Children's Experiences of the Guardian ad litem Service and Public Law Proceedings

Maria Ruegger

Introduction

Guardians ad litem have been charged with representing children's interests in care and related proceedings since May 1984. The statutory provision for the appointment of Guardians was set out in The Children Act 1975 and was implemented in full on 27 May 1984. The duties laid upon Guardians stress the importance of listening to children and conveying their wishes and feelings to the court. It is both important, and consistent with this philosophy, that the future development of the Guardian ad litem service is influenced by the '*consumers*' of that service. Whilst many systems have been developed, both formal and informal, whereby the courts, local authority personnel, lawyers, parents and others provide feedback on the practice of Guardians, no systems yet appear to have evolved whereby children themselves can contribute to knowledge of how the service operates.

However, a number of studies spanning various aspects of the Guardian ad litem and Family Court service have elicited the views of children on their experiences and the service they received (Ruegger, 2001; Hunt and Murch, 1990; Wheal, 1994; Clarke, 1995; Masson and Oakley, 1999; Clarke and Sinclair, 1999). The evidence from these studies points to children having much to contribute to the professional development, not only of Guardians, but also of lawyers, expert witnesses and those responsible for policy development and service delivery at national and local levels.

Research

These research studies were wide ranging, and the extent to which children's views were sought varied according to the main focus of the particular study. This chapter, and indeed this book, has concentrated where possible on the child's perspective. This was also the main focus of a study conducted by the editor, Ruegger, of *Children's Perceptions of the Guardian ad litem Service* during 1997–1999. Forty seven children in two local authorities were interviewed about their experience of the Guardian ad litem service and family law proceedings (see Table 3). This chapter will review the findings of that study and will consider their implications for those whose work brings them into contact with children involved in public law proceedings. Those aspects of the other studies referred to in the first paragraph of this chapter, which are concerned with children's expressed views, are also reported.

Satisfaction with the service

Generally, children expressed a high level of satisfaction with the Guardian service. When asked by Ruegger to describe the Guardian's role, the aspects children mentioned most often were the Guardian listening to them, and explaining court procedures. This finding has been replicated in another recent study (Children's Society, 2000) in which 71 per cent of those interviewed regarded the ability to listen as the single most important quality of the Guardian, whilst 43 per cent considered that the ability to explain legal processes was their most essential attribute. By comparison, the other qualities that the children could have chosen received only a few votes each.

Children talked positively of their experience of having been listened to by people who were interested to know what they thought, and what they wanted to happen. This seemed to be due to their understanding of Guardians being appointed especially to look after their interests, together with the fact that Guardians have no history in the case, and were thus not viewed by children as antagonistic towards their parents. All children across the age groups had a good understanding of that part of the Guardian's role which is concerned with informing the court about their wishes and feelings. The following quotes from the study illustrate the sentiments expressed:

- 'She was perfect.'
- 'If he was someone's best friend they could trust him.'
- 'He comes when you don't know where you will be living in the future.'
- 'I liked having someone I could tell my views to and know that they would be heard by the court.'
- 'Having a Gal helped me a lot—it made me feel secure. I can trust her. At least I had someone to hear me out and listen to me. She was a good listener.'
- 'He wrote it down, exactly as my words, and he said it to the court.'
- 'She was looking out for my interests and spoke to me like an equal.'
- 'He took the time to get to know me and really listened and was interested in me.'

The children interviewed by Clark and Sinclair (1999), were similarly positive about their Guardians:

> *The Guardian's ability to listen was given great prominence ... The children referred to several factors that they used in working out whether they were being listened to. Firstly, there was the manner and personality of the Guardian. Secondly, note-taking was seen by the children as an indication that their views were being taken seriously. Thirdly, evidence*

that the Guardian had taken on board their wishes and feelings by the
answers that were given to specific requests from them.
Clark and Sinclair, 1999.

Some children described how their Guardians had influenced contact arrangements, at their request: others described how the Guardian had helped them get information about family members that they had lost touch with, often siblings.

In the three studies (Clark and Sinclair, 1999; Masson and Oakley, 1999; and Ruegger, 2001) which elicited children's views on the subject of fairness, most children described their Guardian as 'fair to everyone' as well as supportive of themselves. One child commented 'She didn't want me to live with my mum but she did tell what I said to the court: I think she was on both sides' (aged 9). It was important for children to feel that the Guardian was fair to their parents, and a source of anxiety when they did not. Clarke and Sinclair describe the case of a seven year old girl who felt that the Guardian was not fair to her mother, whose distress she was acutely aware of, when it was decided to place her temporarily in foster care during the proceedings.

Guardians were also seen by many children as powerful and influential players, both in the court arena and in resolving disputes with social workers, for example about contact levels. However there was also evidence to suggest that some children were frustrated by their Guardians', and the courts', lack of power to influence the finer detail of the care plan and to intervene in other matters of concern to them. For example, Ruegger reports the views of two brothers who complained that they had been very unhappy in their foster care placement and that their Guardian had not been able to help them. They also said that some of their things had been stolen whilst in foster care and, although their Guardian had written a letter, nothing happened as a result. Another source of much dissatisfaction expressed by children arises from the inability of courts to intervene in matters that concern them most, namely with whom they should live and their contact with family members. Five children in Ruegger's study stated that they wanted their Guardians and the court to make it possible for them to remain with their current short term carers. Great antipathy was expressed in relation to the concept of 'forever families'. One ten year old girl told the researcher that she intended to run away if they tried to take her away from her current 'short term' foster home where she had lived for some 18 months. A twelve year old boy said that he would kill himself before he would move again. Two teenage Asian girls had been placed with agency foster carers, also Asian, on coming into care with their older sister. They were later moved to a county placement with foster carers who did not share their cultural background. The girls were angry about this move and told the researcher that their sister had chosen to return home to an abusive situation rather than remain unhappy in care.

Venues for meetings; privacy and security
All children interviewed across all three studies were seen on at least two occasions by their Guardians, and for periods of from 30 minutes to 90 minutes. The older the child the longer the time they tended to spend with their Guardian. Children were seen in a range of different settings which included their homes, foster homes, residential establishments, schools, adolescent units, restaurants and parks. Ruegger found that children's views about whether a particular venue was a good place to meet appeared to be based on the extent of privacy that could be guaranteed. There was evidence that children preferred being interviewed in their homes, provided that it was possible for interviews to take place without fear of interruption. One nine year old boy who described his bedroom as being a good place to meet gave as his reason, 'I had my computer and my nice comfy bed. I was under the covers when we talked'.

One child said that it made her feel safe to know that her foster carers were in the kitchen when she was talking with her Guardian in another room, and several others drew comfort from the presence of their siblings when they first met their Guardian. Children who met Guardians in their homes talked about the interest shown by the Guardian in their games, photographs and other personal belongings. The fact that Guardians played with children, and showed an interest in them as individuals with interests other than those of proceedings, was frequently commented on.

Several children spoke of how they met with their Guardian in a room which people could have entered at any time. Some expressed their worry that what was said might be overheard by others in adjoining rooms or at other tables in restaurants, and there were several negative comments made about fast food restaurants in this regard. Others drew attention to the privacy that can be had in the booths of some establishments, and in parks. Many of the younger children had also met with their Guardians at school and this was sometimes described as a good place.

However, some children did have strong negative feelings about being seen at school. Clarke and Sinclair draw attention to the importance of asking children where they wanted the visit to take place. 'This choice allowed the child some control over the interview and also told the Guardian a great deal about where the child felt safe.'

Many of the children interviewed had been out for tea with their Guardians and some had been to the park. The children enjoyed these outings but generally seemed to draw a clear distinction between fun times and the business part of their relationship. This is summed up by one child who commented, 'We had fun but the best time was when we were in Auntie Susan's house by ourselves to talk about the court business'.

Both Wheal (1994) and Clarke and Sinclair, drew attention to the importance to children of the timing of meetings. Several children in Wheal's study reported their irritation with Guardians who came to visit when 'Neighbours' was on television. One child told Clarke and Sinclair how she appreciated that the Guardian asked when it was convenient to call, did not make appointments at week-ends and left sufficient time between meetings 'for time to think'.

Most children valued their meetings with their Guardians. Several children commented on the toys that their Guardians made available to them. Others commented positively on the calendars given by Guardians to assist them in understanding the time frame within which proceedings would take place. However, one child complained that every time she wanted to play with the toys, her Guardian would try to talk about the court! Two of the older children suggested that meetings with their Guardian, whilst helpful, did interfere with their social arrangements. Others said that they found some of the questions their Guardians asked them difficult to answer (Ruegger, 2001).

Issues of trust between children and Guardians
Children were asked by Ruegger whether they had felt able fully to confide in their Guardians, and whether they knew what was done with the information they gave her. Whilst most children felt they could confide in their Guardians a great deal, because they knew that the Guardian would relay this information to the judge, nevertheless several spoke of their shock, shame, distress or anger when they discovered that their parents had learnt of their private conversations on receipt of the Guardian's report. Some of these children felt betrayed, and regretted their disclosures: others said that they wished they had been warned in advance. One child specifically stated that the Guardian had told the judge *but not* his mother about the detail of their conversations. He did not appear to realise that his mother would have read the Guardian's report and been present on the occasions on which the Guardian addressed the judge. Several children expressed some degree of unhappiness that things they had said, without knowing they would be repeated to a parent, had been later used against them. In one case, a child said that his parents had blamed the outcome of the proceedings directly on what he had said to his Guardian. Another (aged 10) commented, 'I said I wanted to stay with my Nan. It was hard to say this because you have to be fair to your Mum. I didn't want my Mum to know I said it'.

One child (aged 9), however, indicated that he was aware that the information he gave would have a wider audience than the judge and the Guardian. He commented, 'The Guardian only tells the people he has to (in order) to do something for you'.

Clarke and Sinclair also found evidence of confusion amongst children as to the audience for the Guardian's report:

Whilst some of the children were aware that their families would see the report, others, including one of the older children in the sample, believed that the report was only seen by the judge. This could have been the cause of some difficulties if children were unprepared for possible adverse reaction from members of their family'.

Clarke and Sinclair, 1999.

The message for Guardians, and others who write of children's confidences in court reports and other 'public' documents, appears to be that careful attention should be paid to informing children about what will be done with the information they give, and involving them in decisions about which of the things they do say should appear in reports. Some of the children interviewed by Ruegger had seen, or helped write, the section of the Guardian's report that deals with their wishes and feelings. This group did not appear to be selected on the basis of age. It reflected the preferred working practice of particular Guardians. None of the children who had been involved in these ways felt that their trust had been betrayed.

It is often the case that there is a choice to be made about including information from a child which supports facts that are already well established. Authors, and those they write about, may find that adopting 'the need to know' principle when writing reports will protect some children from allegations of disloyalty and blame for the outcome by disaffected family members, without compromising their duty to convey children's wishes and feelings.

Ascertaining and reporting children's wishes and giving an independent view
A number of children were unaware that the Guardian had a duty to give their own view to the court in addition to representing the child's view. Whilst all children were able to state what the Guardian had told the judge about their wishes, all but eight of the under fourteens were confused about the idea that Guardian would have had anything different to say. In some of these cases, the Guardian had taken a different view from the child. Whilst most of these children indicated that they had written information explaining this aspect of the Guardian's role, and some of them produced the materials that had been given to them by their Guardians that described this aspect of the Guardian's role, they did not seem to have understood that their Guardian had to give a view independent of their own wishes and feelings. The children were always clear about the position taken by other parties although many (almost half) were unaware or unsure of that adopted by their Guardian.

This raises a number of questions. Is the Guardian's role, as representative of the child, so comfortable that some avoid potential conflict with their child clients by choosing to focus on those aspects of their role which are to do with ascertaining wishes and feelings, and minimising those which are concerned with providing the court with an independent recommendation as to outcome? If so, then Guardians may implicitly be making decisions about whether children are old enough to give their own instructions without explicitly stating this. This further raises questions about the role of the child's solicitor, as it is they who ultimately have the responsibility for determining whether the child is competent to give their own instructions. Certainly, solicitors should be aware if there was a difference between the recommendation of the Guardian and the child's expressed wishes. Should solicitors see all their child clients in such circumstances or should they be guided by the Guardian with regard to the competence of the child? It is interesting to note that no child in this study was separately legally represented.

It may be that there is a case for protecting children from being exposed to conflict between themselves and their Guardian, or from being told too much about the court proceedings. Is there such a case to be made and, if so, in what circumstances should Guardians be protecting children? Age might be one factor but there may be others, such as the nature of the particular proceedings or the children's need to retain a positive image of their families.

The evidence from this study suggests that there are variations in Guardian practice with respect to how much information children are given and there are no obvious explanations to account for this. It is possible that 'practice wisdom' may be at work but unless Guardians justify this by debating the issue and making explicit the guidelines that govern practice, such 'wisdom' may potentially operate to the detriment of some children.

Expert witnesses

Twenty-one children saw expert witnesses during the proceedings. The data suggests that children's lack of information about the role of the expert can leave them feeling excluded from, or confused by, the proceedings. Only four children in the study (two in the under 13 group and two in the 14 plus group) who had been assessed by an expert witness, claimed to have knowledge of what the expert had said to the court. There were discrepancies in the data provided by Guardians and children on this point, with Guardians suggesting that children were given much more information than their child clients claimed to have received.

Children across the age range in general felt they had no choice about seeing the expert and eleven were not prepared to do so again if given the choice. Children spoke of their experiences of being taken out of school and brought by a social worker or Guardian to the expert's office. The venues were frequently experienced by the children as 'strange', mostly, it seemed, because the environment was unfamiliar to them.

There was some evidence that teenagers experienced embarrassment at being linked with a psychiatrist. Several young people felt the need to stress that they were not 'mad', and that they had only seen a psychiatrist because the court had said that they must. Another group admitted to seeing an expert for the purpose of the court proceedings but denied that the person they had seen was a psychiatrist. Instead they used terms such as 'counsellor' and 'therapist' to describe the psychiatrist. The ten children, who said that they had been given explanations as to the purpose of meeting with the expert, did not view the experience negatively and all indicated that they would be prepared to meet with the expert again.

Clearly there are implications for Guardians who are working alongside expert witnesses in respect of the desirability and level of the explanations they provide to the children concerned.

It seems that there is a potential for children to experience discomfort, due to the necessarily brief relationship they will have with the expert, and the nature of the discussions they must have with them. This, together with the fact that older children experience distress and embarrassment, arising from associations with the madness label, suggests that Guardians have a responsibility to be clear about the necessity for expert evidence in individual cases. Maybe there is a tension between getting the best available evidence for the court, and the needs of the child who is the focus of the proceedings. In some cases it may be that there is already sufficient evidence; the expert evidence is the icing on the cake, the security blanket for those who are fearful that the court will not recognise their expertise. It may be in the interests of children if Guardians, social workers and the courts were to pay more attention to the 'value added factor'. What can the expert provide that is necessary, within the limitations of the remit of the court, that is not already available from others currently involved? When experts are appointed, Guardians need to become better at explaining to children the nature and purpose of such assessments, and seeking their consent, or, at the very least, their views. They need, also, to have in mind that the child who has been properly prepared for and involved in the assessment will need feedback on the outcome. The evidence from this study suggests that few of the experts are taking on this role at present. Thus, the question of who tells what to the child needs to become a matter for discussion between the expert and those who are in close contact with the child.

Attendance at court

Thirty-nine children reported that they were not consulted about whether they wished to attend court. The Family Proceedings Courts (Children Act 1989) Rules 1991, R11[4] indicates that Guardians should consider with children whether they should attend court and advise the court accordingly. Case law, however, suggests that judges are unlikely to view requests for children's attendance favourably (see for example Re W [1994] The Times, 13 July, Re M (A Minor) (Justices Discretion) [1993] 2 FLR 706 and Re G [1992]. The Times, 19 November). Of the nine children who said they were asked, eight chose to attend, although only one child attended the Final Hearing. This child commented that, despite having obtained prior agreement to sit in on the proceedings, when the day arrived they could not bring themselves to go any further than the waiting room. The others either attended directions Hearings or visited the court building. One child spoke directly with the judge in his chambers. The child in group one who attended court complained that there was no one there when she visited. She said she would like to have attended the Hearing or have spoken to the judge. This child was happy with the outcome, was very clear about her Guardian's role and felt her wishes had been accurately relayed to the court by her Guardian. Several other children said they would have liked the opportunity to speak with the judge. One child wanted to hear what everyone said in court. It is interesting to note that a child's wish to attend court did not appear to be affected by their response to the outcome of proceedings.

Seventeen of the children interviewed said they would like to have attended court, some because they wished for the opportunity to talk directly with the judiciary, others because they wanted to be more involved. They gave as their reasons:

I wanted to see the judges. I don't even know what they look like. I wanted to be there, not in school when they were deciding, and if my mum was upset I could tell her I'll still be seeing you (aged 8).

I would like to see the judge and talk to him and I'll ask him if I can go home to my mum (aged 9).

I would like to go to the court so I could say my own words (aged 8).

I would like to see it because I have never been before and everyone else went when I had to go to school (aged 9).

These children were pleased with the outcome of the proceedings, three having rated the final judicial decision as good, and one as fair. All felt that their needs were being met and that they had been able to confide in their Guardians as to their hopes, wishes and feelings. Yet these children did feel excluded from events at the time of the Final Hearing and were expressing the need to be involved more directly. It is interesting that their wishes did not indicate dissatisfaction with the structures set up to ensure that their views were heard, or a hope that they could have had more influence on the final decision had they been able to express their views directly.

Attendance at court is one aspect of children's experience of public law proceedings that could benefit from further study. In what circumstances should Guardians be asking the court to allow children to attend for all or part of the hearing? Should all children be asked if they wish to attend all or only some parts? If so, what guidelines should Guardians use to assist them to distinguish between such groups? What support, if any, would children need? In what way could attending court be helpful to children? In what circumstances might it be damaging?

Responses to outcomes

The majority of the children said that they thought the decisions made by the court were either good or fair. There was evidence, from the children's responses to the final outcome of proceedings, that many could differentiate between their ideal wishes and the reality of the options open to them. Children were able to convey to Guardians both the difficulties they were experiencing and their wish that relationships could be altered so as to enable them to live happily with their families. They were also accepting of the reality of their situation and prepared to take second best in the form of relief from difficult home circumstances. All but four of the children who did not get their preferred decision from the court understood why, and felt that the court's decision was fair. They gave as their reasons:

They were thinking of sending us back to our dad but we told (the Guardian) our story and she told the judges and they said no.

The court told my family what I needed.

I haven't lost everything, I can still see my mum when I am older.

The expressed wish as stated by all the children who made the above comments was to return home, the outcome was not that, and yet they all rated the decision as fair.

In contrast, the child who was most unhappy at the final outcome did not express a wish to have been in court, although he did ask the researcher if she could tell 'the judges to listen more to the children, as it is they who know best what they need' (aged 9). This child felt that he had said all he could to the Guardian, and that his views had been accurately relayed to the court, but he had concluded that his views had been given no importance by the judge. He was amongst the few children who said they were unhappy with the outcome of proceedings. It is interesting to note that, despite this, he was positive about his relationship with his Guardian ad litem.

Those children who experienced insecurity in their placements expressed dissatisfaction with the outcome of proceedings on the grounds that court orders made were not sufficient to meet their needs. Other dissatisfied children expressed dismay at the gradual reduction of contact with family members which often followed the making of care orders. Whilst they understood the rationale for care orders, and why they could not live with their families, they were less likely to comprehend why they could not continue seeing family members. One child expressed his distress that contact with his mother was going to be reduced from three times weekly to once weekly, then monthly and eventually to three times yearly. Whilst he had anticipated that the court would probably not allow him to live with his mother, he had not been aware that his contact with her would be severely restricted after the proceedings. His distress alerts us to the importance of preparing children for all the likely effects of the court's decisions on their lives, not just the most important or obvious ones.

Conclusion

In summary, the children who have participated in all the studies referred to above expressed many positive views about the Guardian ad litem service. There was evidence that children, generally, felt listened to and supported by their Guardians, and that, through them, they felt able to express their views to the court. That so many children were able to understand and accept decisions which did not accord with their wishes is likely to have been influenced by having the opportunity to explore their circumstances with someone whom they perceived as being on their side, yet fair to all involved.

There was, however, evidence that many children did not fully appreciate who, other than the judge, would learn what they had said to their

Table 3: The sample from whom data was collected

	Under 10	10–13 years	14 plus	Total
Male	5	6	10	21
Female	9	10	7	26
Total	14	16	17	47

Guardians, did not have their agreement sought prior to interview by experts for forensic purposes, and were not informed about the conclusions of any experts they did see. It also emerged that children were often not asked about attendance at court, that they felt frustrated by the Guardian's and the court's lack of power to influence the detail of their care plans, and that they had difficulty understanding the rationale for decisions that were taken about contact. Finally, it seems that children are not as clear as one might expect about the requirement that Guardians give an independent view to the court and that Guardians and solicitors need to carefully consider the circumstances in which separate representation of children may be appropriate. These are almost all matters which Guardians, lawyers and expert witnesses can do something about, in the interests of empowering children and responding to their needs in court proceedings.

Whilst the evidence suggests that children on the whole feel supported and assisted by their Guardians, there are things they can tell us about how we can improve the service we offer. It is my hope that the profession can continue to listen to what children have to say, and thus enable them to contribute to our professional development, as we go forward into CAFCASS.

5 Direct Work with Children

Gillian Norris

Introduction

As a Guardian ad litem myself, I know that the Guardian's role in ascertaining children's 'wishes and feelings' in public Law cases can be a challenge to professional skills, as each child presents a totally different story to transcribe. It can seem particularly problematic at times as guardians must both present the child's views to the court, and also advocate in favour of a decision that is in their best long term interests. Inevitably there are times when these aims can seem to be completely at variance with each other.

Children's powerful emotional ties to parents contribute to most children who are involved in proceedings, wishing that their parent or parents could change and that they could return home to be with them and to be cared for properly. Whatever harm or abuse the child may have endured, they may nevertheless express that what they want is to return to their parents, siblings, pets and all that is most familiar to them. They are often highly sensitive to their parents feelings about the events they have experienced and that have instigated the court's involvement.

The court hearing will, of course, give an opportunity for the possibility of rehabilitation to be considered but for the duration of the proceedings professionals are working with children who are in a transitional situation that is extraordinary and extremely emotive for them.

For the child, being the focus of the process and being listened to, sometimes a novel experience for them, can be empowering and can provide a valued opportunity to participate in the decision-making process of the Court. However, to facilitate children's involvement is, in most cases, not a straightforward task as the harm the child has suffered has impacted on their ability to relate to, and communicate with, friends and adults. Talking about feelings is particularly difficult for children who are unused to be being listened to or who may have had limited opportunities to develop self-confidence and social skills. They may have great difficulty expressing themselves verbally.

A useful evaluation of a child's perspective relies heavily on the professional's ability to build a rapport and to provide resources with which the child can express himself both verbally and non verbally, and share thoughts and concerns. Where a worker is involved over a period of time they not only develop a relationship and talk with the child but also observe the child's behaviour in a variety of settings and try to make sense of what they see or learn from others about them.

Gillian Schofield (1998), urges those working with children to:

> ... *pay attention to how children are thinking, their memories and fantasies, their attributions of blame and responsibility.*

She points out that:

> *There is always a need for an understanding of the psychological complexity of children, but there is a particular need to understand the internal world, the thoughts, wishes and beliefs, of children whose early experiences of neglect or abuse have left them distressed and confused.*

Schofield goes on to remind us that:

> *Betrayal of trust and hurt within the family will severely prejudice a child's capacity to make sense of his experiences. It is essential to bear in mind that it is not only the child's emotional state but also the capacity to make sense of experiences, a cognitive capacity, which is damaged and this will affect the child's capacity to make sense of available options.*

It is the Guardian's role to assist not just the court but the child as well, in trying to make sense of their needs, wishes and feelings, and to present them to the court in a way that gives the child a sense of involvement in the proceedings. In addition to ascertaining the child's views, the child needs our help to understand both how those views have been taken into account during the court hearing and how the judge has come to his decision.

The Boundaries of the Task

There are four identifiable phases to the Guardian's work as far as the child is concerned. The Guardian must:

1. Introduce themselves and help the child to feel confident in the Guardian's ability to listen and get to know them. At this stage it is important to make sure that the child understands the boundaries of the court's task and the limited timeframe of their Guardian's involvement.
2. Try to gain an understanding of the child's world, experiences and any feelings they may have from the past, or from being placed away from family and friends.
3. Share the Guardian's report and recommendations with the child, in a way that makes clear that the child's views are presented and enhances the child's understanding of the court's responsibilities.
4. Explain the court's decision to the child and finally helping the child with saying goodbye to the guardian ad litem in a positive way.

In trying to meet the demands of these tasks I use play and stories as a way of helping children to express themselves. I have found it helpful to use some

of the ideas and resources outlined below as ways of developing a
relationship and of trying to understand the child's inner world.

Some Toys and Games

There are no standard toys or techniques employed by guardians in their
direct work with children. Each has gathered together a collection that
'works for them'. I have used some ideas from the play therapy approach
and put together a variety of toys and games including puppets, soft toys, a
doll's house – play people and furniture, a Russian doll, kaleidoscope, cars
(doctor's, ambulance and police), dominoes, building blocks, and a bag of
sea shells.

Providing a combination of these for interviews usually seems to allow
children the space and support either to talk spontaneously about the things
most troubling them or to depict a scene or dilemma which reflects their
anxieties.

I have also found invaluable, particularly for younger children, a book
from The Children's Society, *Meeting Your Guardian ad litem* (1992) which
explains the Guardian's role through a story about a rabbit. I take with me
a soft toy rabbit that can be held by me or the child as I read the story. I
also keep a collection of photocopies of pictures and worksheets which can
be used as part of a book we can put together about their situation during
the course of the proceedings.

One is often seeing children in an adult space: their family home or the
foster placement or possibly in a teacher's room at school. However, by
taking the same folder each time, together with the child's Court Calendar[1],
and the same toys, the child is reminded that we are meeting to focus on
their situation, and some continuity is offered which helps the child to link
up with the play, talks and thoughts already shared.

An Example

I shall now describe some direct work that I engaged in with a child for
whom I was appointed guardian in order that the nature of the activity and
the process are made clear. The case described below is unusual in that it
involved a more extensive level of direct work than is often the case. My
involvement was over a period of six months and during that time I filed five
court reports.

The background

The children's mother had been known to social services and other agencies
for many years because of the impact on her parenting of the mental illness

---

[1] The Hertfordshire Court Calendar, produced by the Hertfordshire Panel of Guardians ad litem
is a large colourful calendar with information about the guardian's role explained in child
friendly language. The child can enter the dates of court hearings, along with other important
dates and thereby gain an understanding of the timeframe for the proceedings.

from which she suffered, and for which she had undergone many months of in-patient treatment. The children had required several periods of voluntary care which were followed by rehabilitation to their mother. There were long standing concerns about the very serious neglect from which the children had been suffering. For example, there were frequent referrals from neighbours and community agencies about the children appearing hungry, unsuitably dressed, playing unsupervised in the street and missing school or nursery. Friends, family and professionals had been, along with social services, offering help and support to the mother in order to try to keep her family together, but her problems showed little improvement over a period of two years. Social services decided that the children now needed a settled, long term placement rather than further attempts at rehabilitation, and in the light of this instituted care proceedings.

In the past the mother had always worked with social workers towards the children returning home. She did not accept that there was a need for social services to have statutory responsibility for her children and she contested at each stage during the care proceedings. However, at the conclusion of the case she was in fact in agreement with the care plan, which was for a permanent alternative family, and consented to the making of an order.

The child

Tara was the elder of two girls who had, by the time I was appointed as their Guardian, been in and out of foster placements over a period of nearly four years. Tara was aged six and her sister aged four, and they had until recently been expecting that once again when their mother was better they would return home. They had no knowledge of their father. The only other adults they knew well were the maternal grandfather, who was now too ill to be of assistance, and their mother's boyfriend, who had recently moved into the family home.

It was clear from the statement in support of the local authority's applications for care orders that the mother's mental illness had become more severe since the birth of the younger child and that Tara had, since the age of two, often acted as her mother's helper and taken on caring responsibilities far beyond her years. She presented as a little adult who was eager to please and who could talk on equal terms with any one. She had refused to see her mother for contact the previous week after being told by her on the telephone that she was to be adopted and would never see her again. She spoke as if she knew her own mind.

There were disagreements about many things reportedly said to the children which, it was considered, had contributed to Tara presenting as a worryingly disturbed youngster who at times refused to eat, and would sit or stand still, as if frozen, for long periods of time: on her bed, at the door of the sitting room or under the tree in the garden. At school Tara was stealing food, was said to be 'attention seeking' and was thought to be over friendly to strangers.

Introductions
In the first interview, which took place during May, Tara said she was happy
to listen to the story *Meeting your Guardian ad litem*, and then to do some
colouring (her favourite occupation). In the middle of the story however, she
told me she had something to say. She went to the centre of the room and
said she didn't want to see Mummy because 'she makes me stand still and
tells me not to eat'. She went on to list a number of household tasks her
mother made her do, washing her hair, hoovering and washing up, and then
she returned to sit down.

   After the story I explained to Tara that what she had said to me would
be communicated to the Judge when I next saw him. I also told her that he
would hear from a number of people, including her mother, before he made
a decision about what should happen, both about contact and about matters
to do with her future care.

   Before the next interim hearing I saw Tara at school and also observed a
contact between her mother and her sister. (Tara had refused to attend for
the second time.) At school she was happy to hear the 'rabbit' story again
and to draw a picture of her family which we would use as the first page of
the book we would put together. She seemed to flourish with individual
attention; she was chatty and forthcoming and she explained to me how she
liked to keep busy, doing sums, colouring and reading. About contact she
was clear that she had refused to go 'because of Mummy saying things'.

   Tara told me she was willing to go to contact with her sister, if it was held
at the family centre and supervised by a social worker in the way that I had
described.

Contact Hearing mid June
At this stage concerns about Tara's eating had increased. The contact
arrangements were that Tara should have one supervised session a week with
her mother at the family centre. She continued to decline the chance to
attend. At the foster placement her periods of frozen rigidity were increasing,
and her mood was flat and unresponsive. A report from a child psychiatrist
identified her as traumatised and in need of psychotherapy.

   I saw Tara again at school as I had sensed that she felt more at ease there
than at the foster placement. Tara enjoyed reading the 'rabbit' story to me
this time, and afterwards we played a game, *All about Me* (Barnardos, 1991).
This helped her to share what her favourite drinks and foods were, what pets
and animals she liked and to tell me that best of all she wished she could be
a mum, and look after her sister Sarah.

   When she talked about her mother and contact, she was clear that she did
not want to see her. She said she didn't like her because she tells her 'not to
eat and to sit still'.

Contact Hearing end of June
In my next report, I pressed for social services to arrange for the foster carers
to be given advice by the child psychiatrist and requested that the contact

arrangements, once a week, supervised, at the family centre, continue as before with Tara having the option of attending with her sister. The report was for a contested contact hearing at which the mother's application for increased contact was upheld. An order was made increasing supervised contact to twice a week, and the Judge made it clear that it should be explained to Tara that she was expected to go to contact. Although I had opposed the application for an order for increased contact, it was decided that as Guardian ad litem I should be the one to tell the children of the judge's decision.

I visited Tara at the foster home the next day and was shocked to see her looking so dejected and withdrawn. She sat as if frozen in the chair, her shoulders and head down, her hands clasped together in her lap and she made no eye contact. After acknowledging how sad she looked, I gently asked her if she would be willing to look at the book we had started to put together and some of the pictures she had coloured. She responded, but in a flat tone and then read each word slowly and deliberately, like a much younger child. She agreed then to build up a family house picture with me (*Make a Scene*, 1998), and we sat on the carpet together.

She began to engage with the activity, seeming to enjoy the mechanical nature of it, and, after receiving lots of praise and encouragement, she became gradually more at ease and forthcoming. I then reminded her about the book we had read together (*Meeting Your Guardian ad litem*), and about the rabbit in a muddle. I explained that I'd seen the Judge the day before. Tara was fully engaged at this stage and had entered into the puppet and toy play set up that I used, as judge and child, with obvious enjoyment.

Through the puppets we played out how I had spoken to the Judge about what she had told me, and how he had also listened to her mother and had decided that there should be contact. I told her that the Judge had asked me to tell her that he would really like her to go to contact. She listened carefully and acknowledged that she understood. When I suggested I call the foster carer to go over what we'd talked about, Tara immediately removed herself back to the armchair and, with head down and shoulders stooped looked completely dejected again. She was able to tell her carer of our work together but was monosyllabic and flat in tone. Clearly this was very concerning and emphasised, to my mind, the need for the carer to work closely with the child psychiatrist.

A week later things were completely different; Tara's attitude had changed. She spoke to her mother on the phone and did go to contact. She continued to attend contact sessions for the duration of the proceedings.

Mother's application for a Residential Assessment (Children Act 1989, section 38.6)

A month later Tara's mother applied for a residential assessment in respect of which there was a request for another expert to interview the children. I opposed the involvement of another expert but, as the Judge was minded to hear the mother's case, he requested that the children be interviewed by the

Guardian in the presence of the expert rather than introduce yet another professional assessor to the children.

It was arranged that I would interview the children at the family centre and ask six questions that had been formulated by the expert. The children were prepared by me at the foster placement, using the same soft toys as before, to explain the Judge's suggestion.

At the family centre I used three play houses to indicate the family home, the foster placement and the assessment unit. (Both children were aware from telephone contact that their mother wanted to take them to an assessment centre.) Tara's sister played normally and did colouring for her folder. With the toy rabbit on my knee, I asked Tara the six questions as though she were having a conversation with the toy rabbit, and as if the rabbit may be going to live at home with her mother.

This seemed to provide a safe space for Tara to talk freely about her own and her sister's early experiences, and although some of it was painful for myself and the expert to hear, Tara herself was not upset. She seemed to enjoy being able to 'help' the rabbit and the rabbit helped her to express and communicate many of her feelings. One of the things that also emerged was that she was now enjoying the contact with her mother, and that she was pleased that she'd 'been going every time since our talk'.

I filed a copy of my account of this interview with my next interim report in the hope that this would assist the court to understand Tara's past experiences of being parented. I also filed a copy of accounts of two contact sessions Tara had recently attended as these gave an indication of the nature of the relationship between mother and child. They showed how Tara behaved as her mother's friend and confidant rather than as a child, and how the insensitivity of her mother towards her more childlike feelings often left Tara feeling rejected, which in turn impacted on her self esteem. I opposed the mother's section 38(6) Application because of the high risk, in my view, of failure of a residential assessment and the likely detrimental effect this would have on the children. After reading all the reports the mother sought, and was granted, leave to withdraw her Application. The parties agreed that I should tell the children of the outcome.

Time for straight talking

At the foster placement both girls were anxious and clearly waiting to hear about what had happened at court. Through contact and telephone calls with their mother they were very aware of the hearing, and of their mother's understandable preoccupation with it. In their state of expectation they seemed to want to be straightforward and although the owl and rabbit were on my lap, the children asked me to tell them directly what the Judge had said.

I told them that the Judge had listened very carefully to everyone but although he had understood that their mummy loves and cares about them, he had decided that, as she really is quite ill sometimes and can't look after them properly, they should not go away with her to the assessment centre.

I explained that they would stay at the foster placement. We then sat on the floor together whilst the children did some colouring for their books. As they were thinking things through they asked questions, and sought reassurances, about what it had been like in court and how their mother had reacted.

Tara was able to say whilst colouring that she was 'a bit sad and a bit happy,' sad that she wasn't going to live with Mummy and 'a bit happy' that she would see her at the family centre. She explained her mixed feelings about living away from Mum by saying 'It's the feeling that it's different living here (with the foster carer) and it's not different living with Mummy'.

The foster carer reported a few days later that Tara seemed relieved that a decision had been taken and that she was attending and returning cheerfully from contact.

Thinking with others about the future

Before the Final Hearing in December, Tara's mother continued to contest the making of a care order as she did not agree with the social services plans to seek adoptive parents for the two girls and to discontinue her contact with them.

Tara and her sister needed the commitment that mature adoptive parents could offer and, with the court-appointed child psychiatrist, I sought to persuade the local authority of the importance of an adoption placement with openness. It was accepted by this stage that both children had severe attachment disorders and, as a consequence, that they had deeply ambivalent and confused feelings about their mother.

There was no benefit to Tara of knowing about the tangled web of discussions and negotiations which took place at this stage. The reviewed care plans presented at the Final Hearing reflected the local authority's intention to seek adopters who would consider an open approach to contact, and also an agreement for continuation of contact until such time as the children were permanently placed.

After the Final Hearing I visited the children to tell them what the Judge had decided, and to describe how things had gone at court. Once again they wanted directness and to know who was with their mum and how she had been. I showed them the report I had written and read to them individually the paragraphs that described their wishes and feelings. Tara knew from this that I had spoken to the Judge about how important supervised contact with her mother was to her.

I read once again the story about the rabbit so that they could recognise that our work together was nearly complete. This helped to prepare them for saying goodbye, and we used some time to finish the pictures for their books and folders.

Endings

For the final interview I finished and put together for each child the book that we had been writing throughout our meetings about the court case, and included an explanation of the outcome of the proceedings. A copy of Tara's book is reprinted in full at the end of this chapter. I also compiled their drawings, the Court Calendar and worksheets into a Guardian Service document folder used by Hertfordshire Panel of Guardians ad litem. I visited the children at the foster placement and we sat on the carpet to read through each book, and we then looked through all the pictures in their folders. I thanked them for all their hard work with me and suggested they might want to keep the books and folders somewhere safe. The handing over of the books and letters to the children symbolised the completion of our task so that we could say our good-byes. The books helped the children understand the reasoning behind the Judge's decision and would assist them in the future should they wish to clarify their memories about all that had happened and the reasons why.

Like so many of the children who are the subjects of public law proceedings, Tara and her sister were in the unhappiest of situations. Their initial wish for reunification with their mother was not going to be the happy end to their story. The social services care plan for an alternative permanent family was undoubtedly, in my view, the 'least detrimental alternative, despite there being no certainty that the children would be found an adoption placement, or when this would be. In fact some months later I was told that concerns about the foster placement had escalated and that the children had moved to another more mature and experienced carer. Hopefully the work undertaken with the children during the proceedings would have given them sufficient understanding of their own and their mother's situation to make sense of what was happening, and the regular contact with her would allow them to trust that there can be continuity in a meaningful relationship, even where there are major changes in their care arrangements.

Conclusion

Even though the Guardian ad litem can have no part in ensuring the plans agreed are followed through it is rewarding to be able to work with children, to be able to help them find a voice and to take part in ensuring that their feelings and views are heard and taken into account. However contested the case and overwhelming the challenge of advocating on their behalf, it is, I find, always a privilege to be involved in a decision making process that recognises and prioritises children's needs and seeks to enhance their childhood experiences.

Tara's Book
For Tara

Chapter 1

This is your book to help you understand why you are living with Linda and David at the moment.

My name is G . . . N. . .

I have a job with a very difficult name.

I am called a Guardian ad litem.

I am your Guardian ad litem.

This means I am a special kind of friend who will come to see you for a little while.

I have to help people decide what is the best way to keep you safe.

I would especially like to know what you think.

I shall probably come to see you over a period of a few months.

I shall also talk to other people like Mummy, Grandad and the social workers.

When I have done that I will write a letter to the Judge, who is very clever at understanding muddles like the one in your family.

All the grown ups, including Mummy, will have a chance to talk to the Judge about the worries Angela and the other social workers had when you lived at home.

Chapter 2

When I saw you it seemed that you understood why people were worried and also that Mum had been ill. I could see that it had been very hard for you and that you had always tried your hardest to be helpful to your Mum and to your sister.

I think this is too much for a little girl of six and that all the worries were not good for you.

When we talked together you told me about your upset feelings from things that Mum had said.

You really didn't want to see her but you knew that Sarah did. I thought that it was very kind and helpful of you to think about Sarah's feeling's so carefully.

I know you felt Linda and David looked after you well but you seemed, I thought, to miss belonging in a family.
I told the Judge what your feelings were and because he knew how hard Mum was trying to put things right again, he asked if you would please go to contact sessions with her again so he could try to work out the best way forward for you and Sarah.
It was very helpful of you, that you did after that, go to contact sessions. I think maybe it helped that it was always at the family centre with a social worker there.
I was there sometimes too and also other people who were trying to help the Judge work out what plans would be best for you and Sarah.
I showed you the long letter I wrote for the Judge so that he could understand your life story properly. I told him how muddled the situation was for you and how loyal you were.
You did not specially want to see Mum more, you told me, and I explained to him as well that you were happy that he was going to decide what was best for you.
I also told him what I thought would be best.

Chapter 3

After hearing from everybody in Court the Judge decided that you and Sarah will not be going to live with Mum as she often is ill and her illness stops it. He and everyone in Court recognised that when she is not well she is not able to look after you properly.
It is important to remember that Mum loves you but also knows that she cannot look after you properly and that is why she wants you to be looked after by someone else.
It was agreed by everyone in Court that there will be contact.
I talked about contact a lot with the special worry doctors who had seen you and also your solicitor, B . . . R. It was something thought about very carefully.
You will stay with Linda and David at the moment. Your social worker will look for a new family for you to belong to: for always, not just for a while, like Linda's.
It will be a family for both you and Sarah together.

I remember telling you what the Judge had decided and saw that you were very concerned about how your Mum was afterwards.

You were reassured when I told you that she had been there with Shane and her Barrister and that she had been very brave.

Angela, your social worker will be talking to you a lot about all this.

Sometimes this will make you feel sad.

Sometimes you might feel worried.

Sometimes you might feel pleased.

However you feel, you can always talk to Angela or Linda about it, or, later on to your new Mum and Dad.

I have enjoyed coming to see you and I hope this book helps you to understand our work together and what the Judge has thought about in making his decision.

You might want to keep it so that you can read it again later on.

I hope that you will be very happy in your new family when Angela has found the right one for you both.

With best wishes,
Gillian, your Guardian ad litem.

6 Attachment Versus Black Identity: Balancing Components of the Welfare Checklist in Assessing the Needs of Black Children

Julia Hughes

Introduction

A complex process is involved in balancing the needs of young black children in trans-racial foster placements. A decision to move a child from a trans-racial placement is highly controversial; in reaching such a decision, it is necessary to balance the emotional harm that might be caused by disrupting an existing attachment, against the damage caused by failure to provide for the child's identity needs with regard to race, religion and culture.

In my experience as a Guardian ad litem, black children who have been placed trans-racially as babies are often left to drift in these placements. These are usually emergency short term placements where it is considered, in my opinion wrongly, that matching according to a child's race, religion and culture is less important for a younger child. Once these placements drift, the debate rages whether attachment takes precedence over identity. This trend is supported by Kirton's findings (2000).

A depth of understanding is required about the needs of black children in care; of the arguments for and against trans-racial placements, of the process involved to enable a black child to develop and maintain a healthy black identity, as well as an understanding of the political context within which racism operates. The following chapter will include an historical overview of the debate on 'same-race' placements, and the meaning and importance of issues of race and identity will also be explored as they relate to black children. The chapter will be written with case material in mind and will examine the process of balancing the components of the Welfare Checklist, set out in the Children Act 1989, in assessing the needs of young black children.

The Children Act 1989 was significant in defining the manner in which social services met the needs of black children, placing a new duty on local authorities to give 'due consideration to' a 'child's racial origin and cultural and linguistic background,' in making decisions about them (Children Act, 1989: Barn *et al.*, 1997). To some degree the Children Act enshrined the same-race placement policy (placing black children with carers of the same ethnic group). This debate has now even greater relevance with the publication of the Macpherson Inquiry Report (1999) after the racist murder of Stephen Lawrence. The report has placed 'race' back onto the political agenda, in particular with its definition of institutional racism which has significance in all aspects of public services (Hughes 2000).

Some Definitions

Any debate on issues relating to race necessitates an explanation on the choice of terms and terminology used within this chapter. The term 'race' has been variously defined, and is commonly and inaccurately substituted by terms such as ethnicity, culture and nationality (Spencer and Markstrom-Adams, 1990) Gilroy describes races as 'imagined, socially and politically constructed, which contribute and are tied to uneven patterns of class formation, rather than simple expressions of either biological or cultural sameness, which have been integral to modern racial typology and white supremacy' (1993). It is this definition of race which the author employs here.

The term 'black' is used here to refer to a population within Britain who is liable to be subjected to racism on the basis of their skin colour.

It is important to recognise that racism impacts differently on different groups of black children; it is therefore necessary to distinguish between different groups to illustrate some of these differences. 'Black of dual heritage' is the term used here to describe blacks who are direct offspring of a black relationship between a black and a white person, since it is one of the more positive and least derogatory terms that exist for this social category. A significant example of the impact of the way in which racism operates in social work is the high number of black African, African-Caribbean and children of dual heritage in the care system, whilst children of South Asian origin tend to be under represented (Brophy, 2000).

Trans-racial Adoption . . .?

The issue of trans-racial adoption has become a moral minefield. To many it has become the symbol of institutional racism (Laurance, 1983). The two opposing sides take very different starting points in their argument: those that argue **against** trans-racial placements take a political perspective, considerating the global impact of racism on the individual, whereas those who argue **in favour** of trans-racial placements take a more individualistic approach, using research of small samples with questions based on the Coopersmith (1967) 50-item self esteem inventory to demonstrate their argument.

A trans-racial placement is defined as the placement for fostering or adoption 'by parents (usually of white, European origin) of an ethnically different child, usually of Afro-Caribbean origin' (Bagley and Young, 1993).

This was a practice considered 'normal' and 'unproblematic' in the 1960s under the guise of an apparently non-racial system and in keeping with a commitment to racial integration (Stubbs, 1987). At this time the number of black children in care was low but on the increase and there was little debate about their placement needs. Trans-racial placements were and continue rather naively to be regarded by some as an 'optimistic blending and sharing of ethnic group cultures and heritages' (Bagley, 1993). This argument fails to take into account the nature of power in families since power is not held by children, it is held by adults, who dictate the style of the family.

Supporters of trans-racial placements claim that since 80 per cent of the white British population hold marked non-prejudiced and accepting views of black people and their culture, trans-racially placed children would be unlikely to be placed with racist parents (Bagley, 1993). Several major studies have researched trans-racial placements in the United Kingdom and America, and the overall message emerging from them is that they are largely successful and that trans-racially placed children grow up to become well-balanced individuals, undamaged by the experience. The studies include those undertaken by Gill and Jackson (1983), Bagley (1993), Simon and Alstein (1987), Tizzard and Phoenix (1993) and more recently Thoburn, Narford and Rashid (1999), all of whom have conducted similar studies. They have concluded that there was no evidence to show that being a black child in a white family caused significant maladjustments in the child and that there were 'generally good psychological outcomes in terms of a number of standardised measures of adjustment' (Bagley and Young, 1993). Simon and Alstein (1987) demonstrate how fervent the debate becomes concluding, that 'refusing to consider trans-racial adoption violates a basic tenet in the field of social work'.

Tizzard and Phoenix claim that these children have 'at least as high a level of self-esteem as white adopted children; that they tend to have good relations with their adopted parents and with their peers, and that they have no more behaviour problems than white adoptive children' (1993). Further, they conclude that 'the ethnicity of the parents is less important than the parents' ideological standpoint on racism.' They question what they see to be the heart of the argument of the opponents of trans-racial adoption, namely that of the concept of 'black identity' (1989).

Thoburn, Norford and Rashid claim that despite 'the best endeavours of their parents, some trans-racially placed children suffered additional stress as a result of losing contact with their racial and cultural origins as well as with their birth families' (1999). McRoy and Zurcher's study (1983) gives some evidence of some of the pressures placed on trans-racial adoptees and their families when dealing with racism in their communities, extended families and schools. They describe the greater ease of same-race adoptions demonstrating that same-race adopters are more likely to use racial designations in self-description and that there is often evidence of discomfort on the part of trans-racial adoptees in relating to other black people. They conclude that 'most of the trans-racial adoptive parents were preparing their children to live in a white society,' and that 'only some of these families will be able to fulfill the child's needs to feel positively about his or her racial group identity'.

. . . Or Same Race Adoption?

Those who consider that trans-racial placements are not in the interests of black children include Hayes who questions some of the contradictions of these empirical studies, all of which he claims are similar in research design and remarkably similar in their conclusions (1993). Kirton provides an excellent analysis of all the studies undertaken thus far, claiming that the research promotes an oversimplified view of experiences within trans-racial adoption. Kirton argues that the thorny ethico-political questions are rarely touched upon. He claims that the psychological tests used to promote the argument are 'far too crude a device for tackling the complexities of adoptive identities' and that the implication in these studies is that identity problems experienced by trans-racial adoptees would 'be both severe and readily detectable' (2000). This view is supported by Barn (1999) and Cohen (in Gaber and Aldridge, 1994). Barn claims that measures used to provide indicators for the measurement of black identity are 'highly subjective and value laden' (1999).

Kirton considers that:

> *a distinction must be drawn between that which requires ongoing black contact and solidarity and that which can be internalised by the child in such a way as to work outside such relations . . . Thus while many white people will recognise the existence of racism as a social force, appreciation of its emotional depth is likely to be quite rare as is acquaintance with black pain and searching self-reflection on whiteness . . . Judgements on racism do have to be made in relation to adoption policy and practice, this involves notions of children's needs in respect of racism and the capacities of parents to meet them . . . what should be clear is that the need for a 'secure base' from which to explore issues of identity remains as important as ever, as does that for collectivity and access to strong minority ethnic networks' (2000).*

Kirton argues that there continues to be powerful evidence of the existence of racism in all aspects of society, which demonstrates how deeply ingrained racism is; it should follow therefore, 'that adoption policy for minority ethnic children should 'follow' rather than 'advance' any developments in the decline of racism (2000). Pennie (1987), supports this view that politics cannot be divorced from meeting the needs of black children.

Proponents of same-race placements in Britain believe that white families are not aware of the omnipresence of racism, and its effects, that they have difficulty in dealing with it themselves and are not adequately equipped to provide the child with the skills to survive in a hostile society. They claim that when confronted with racism in such an environment the child's self-esteem can be affected, causing severe psychological damage and 'identity confusion', which the families are then unable to deal with (ABSWAP, 1983; Small, 1984; Pennie, 1987; BAAF, 1995)

To deny the existence of racism is, according to Boyd-Franklyn, 'to misguide the psycho-educational development of the child. No matter if the child is insulated from the overt personal confrontations with racism, the vestiges of racist society are omnipresent' (McAdoo, 1985). Further, it ignores the written testimony of blacks who lived through such experiences, and rejects what has been established independently regarding the nature of the self-concept (Davey, 1987). In promoting this argument, case illustrations are advanced to demonstrate the harmful emotional impact that some black children suffer as a result of being trans-racially placed. Such examples do not appear to feature in the arguments of those who promote trans-racial placements. The most alarming of these examples are attempts by such children to bleach or scrub their skin white, in the vain attempt to resemble their adoptive families and escape the racism with which they have difficulty dealing. Such illustrations lead to the core of the debate and the issue that particularly concerns guardians when balancing the needs of black children: the impact of a trans-racial placement on the child's identity and identity development and the likelihood that being in a trans-racial placement can cause the child emotional harm.

Developing Identity

BAAF places great emphasis on the importance of a positive racial identity stating that a child's primary needs are 'love security and continuity of care ... over and above these basic needs children need to develop a positive identity, including a positive racial identity' (1995). Barn (1999) states that 'the psychological concept of identity is an elusive one. When 'race' and culture are added to the equation, the academic debate becomes even more complex'. Gilroy takes a socio-political constructionist approach to define black identity formation. He regards this as an 'infinite process' and identifies blackness as an open signifier which allows for the possibility of pluralised conceptions of black identities. Gilroy labels this approach 'syncretic', where the nexus for the formation of any black identity is based on a conscious and unconscious construction of raw materials of experience; these include both biological and material factors, such as one's body, family, social networks, and community and the meanings attached to these, as well as ideological factors, such as social, cultural, racial and political discourse, which attempt to give meanings to the social divisions in society (Gilroy, 1993).

Richards in Gaber and Aldridge (1993) defines our understanding of identity as involving 'a strong component of sameness. Identity rests on a commonality with others, on a sharing of experience or attribute. Our identities depend on us identifying with something larger than ourselves, whether it be nation, gender, religion, class, region, language or something else; an individual's identity will include a synthesis of a number of such identifications'. Katz (1996) argues that 'racial identity is inseparable from personal identity,' and that 'early parenting and attachments do not create or determine late identity in a simple cause-effect relationship; early parenting may be a creation of later 'identity' rather than 'identity' being a product of parenting patterns'. It is therefore clear that the environment in which a child lives, is crucial for the development of a healthy black identity.

Moore, in Spencer *et al.* (1985), found that black children adopted by black families 'displayed higher levels of social and emotional adjustment than did black children adopted by white families'. Ince's study (1999) found evidence that trans-racial placements exposed most of the young people (in her study) 'to overt and covert forms of racism and discrimination . . . In the absence of protective mechanisms and supportive frameworks' trans-racially adopted children 'were unable to develop positive coping strategies'. Howe and Feast (2000) found that being trans-racially placed presented black children with additional and more difficult challenges in their search for a fuller sense of identity.

It is already widely known that the fact of being adopted, involves a number of painful emotional issues for children. Howe and Feast's research examines why children search for their natural parents. They identify that the motivation that induces adoptees to search for their roots includes 'the wish to develop a more complete sense of identity' (2000). It therefore should follow that if many adopted children consider that they lack a sense of identity as a consequence of being adopted, then this would become more acute for children whose visible distinction from their families on the basis of their race, culture and ethnicity has been obvious since being placed with them.

A number of psychologists and psychiatrists who have come across children who have been trans-racially placed consider that these children will experience identity problems at some stage in their childhoods. Banks and Maxime see the problems as occurring in early childhood. BAAF, Small, Barn and Rose see them as manifesting in adolescence (Katz, 1996).

The Contribution of Environment to Identity

In considering the needs of black children the impact of the environment on the child's identity is crucial. This is particularly the case if the child is placed in a location where the culture, language, religion and race would be incongruous to that of the child's heritage. Consideration needs to be given as to whether the identity that is created as a result of that placement would be so incongruous as to make it difficult for the child to be accepted by the wider society and particularly by other blacks. An example of this that I have come across was where a black child of Jamaican heritage was placed with white foster carers who then moved to live with the child in rural Ireland. The child was then likely to acquire a religion, language, culture and dialect that was completely incongruous with its racial, linguistic cultural and religious origins. The identity that would be created as a result of that placement would cause the child considerable difficulties in being accepted by its own community of origin as well as the community in which it was brought up.

Johnson and Sherman (1987), found that while many of their families initially felt it to be important to maintain links with the black community, they could not make the final commitment to altering their lifestyles. 'They minimised the importance of race, their children's experience of racism wanting them to 'identify themselves with the 'human race', or as 'black and white' . . . about half of the parents described their children as periodically troubled by their racial difference from other family members'. Research has frequently found that the adoptive parents of trans-racially placed children 'make only limited efforts to give their children a sense of pride and awareness about their heritage' (King, 1993). It is important to consider this when making recommendations that, despite good intentions to actively promote black children's identities by maintaining links with the black community, this is unlikely to be sustained in the longer term.

In making recommendations about whether a child should remain in a trans-racial placement, a thorough assessment of the carers should cover the following: the adoptive families' motivation to adopt, their understanding of the processes involved in racism and their strategies for dealing with it as a family, the environment they live in and whether this environment is racially, ethnically and culturally compatible with the child's. It must not automatically be assumed that all black communities are homogenous, since different communities have a different experience of racism. For example recently arrived refugee communities from Somalia or the Congo are likely to have a different understanding and experience of racism in Britain and should not necessarily be promoted as positive role models to support the development of a healthy black identity for a child of Caribbean heritage.

It is important to discover how accepting the family is of the child's heritage and what strategies they have to promote and enhance the child's identity. The composition of the family and whether or not the adopted child will be isolated within that family, becomes more significant if the adoptive child is the only black child of a number of siblings. Also vital is the consideration that is given to the impact which having a black child will have on the family and on any natural children they might have, since research has shown that white children can often be stigmatised and derided because they have a black adopted sibling.

In assessing the motivation of adopters to care for a black child, it is important to measure the significance that they attach to a child's need for a black identity. How does one judge a carer who places race, religion and culture at the bottom of any hierarchy of needs, when this is in competition with attachment? Ratna Dutt (1998) considers that there is a difference between the responses of black carers and white carers in considering the importance of race, religion, language and culture to a child's life, and therefore that black carers are therefore more able to help and support a black child moving on to a more appropriate placement.

BAAF in their practice notes (1995) stress that a substitute white carer of a black child should have 'additional qualities over and above those needed in nurturing a white child'. A placement that has arisen simply as a result of being an emergency short term placement is therefore less likely to have such qualities. In such cases the carers are more likely to have been assessed as short term carers, and are likely to have been specifically assessed to care for white children rather than black children. Their knowledge of the issues involved in caring for a black child will therefore not have been tested. Any learning and knowledge are likely therefore to have taken place only once the child has been placed.

The Importance of the Child's Age and Attachment

Other aspects of the Welfare Checklist, such as the age of the child and the quality of its attachment are vital in determining the question of placement. It is widely known that the younger the child is when placed for adoption, the better the chances of success. Howe's research (1998) is invaluable in this area; he cites that children who are older than six months when placed, have an increased risk of mental health, behavioural and psychiatric problems. The age of a child at placement is also an important factor in the risk of disruption. 'Breakdown rates range between five and fifteen per cent for children placed under ten years old but rise steeply, sometimes reaching 40–50 per cent for children placed after the age of twelve or thirteen years', according to Howe. Howe cites McWhinnie's research which indicates that if a child experiences more than one change of home before being placed, the chances of a successful adoption are reduced (1998). The quality of the child's attachment is of most significance in determining the success of any adoptive placement. If the child is securely attached, it is more likely to be able to transfer that attachment, improving the chances of a successful placement. Thoburn and Sellick (1996) similarly identify the variables associated which increase the likelihood of disruption. These include whether or not a child has been able to form a secure and positive attachment, if it is under the age of five, does not have a history of abuse, and has not experienced multiple moves.

An important aspect of the equation are the child's wishes and feelings and its ability to express these. The child's age and understanding of the situation and the impact of any change to the child, both in the short, medium and long-term are also vital.

Finding Black Families

One of the arguments often used to justify trans-racial placements has been that black families are hard to recruit for black children and that waiting for appropriate placements has a negative impact on children (Howe and Feast 2000). The Local Authority Circular, *Adoption Achieving the Right Balance* (1998) weighs heavily against children languishing in care when this is due to an inability to locate the most appropriate cultural, racial and religious match for the child. The circular appears to signal a departure from same-race placement by diluting the importance of matching children according to their ethnicity and religion, insisting that 'ethnic origin and religion . . . are, however, only some among a number of other significant factors and should not of themselves be regarded as the decisive ones' (1998). It insists 'the Government has made it clear that it is unacceptable for a child to be denied loving adoptive parents solely on the grounds that the child and adopters do not share the same racial or cultural background' (1998).

In coming to a recommendation about moving a child, other variables need to be considered such as delay and the time scale involved in locating an appropriate placement. BAAF in its Practice Note 18 (1991) seeks to explode the myth that black families cannot be found for black children. It was and continues to be the case that preconceived ideas about the narrow concept of what a family is, lack of knowledge about how and where to recruit black families as well as a resistance by some local authorities (for financial reasons) to using private agencies to locate families specifically for a child has caused delay and drift in placing black children with families who meet their physical and emotional needs as well as their ethnic, cultural, religious and racial needs.

Brophy in her recent research confirms the complexity of many of these cases, which is evidenced by the fact that cases concerning black children and children of dual heritage are more likely to be transferred to the High Court. The question of whether or not a child should be moved from a trans racial placement has been dealt with variously by the Courts and appears to depend largely upon which judge hears the case and the weight that is placed upon the child's identity needs. In *Re N (A Minor) (Adoption)* [1990] 1 FLR 58, the detrimental impact of racism on the child, and the child's needs for a black identity are dismissed. In his judgement Judge Bush contends: 'I have no wish to enter into what is clearly a political field: the emphasis on colour rather than cultural upbringing can be mischievous and highly dangerous when you are dealing in practical terms with the welfare of children'.

In contrast *Re P (A Minor) (Adoption)* [1990] 1 FLR 96, the Court of Appeal held that the judge had 'been entitled, after hearing the evidence, to conclude that the advantages of bringing up a child of mixed race in a black family outweighed the importance of maintaining the status quo for a child who was thriving in a stable home with a white foster mother'. See also *Re O (Transracial adoption: contact)* [1995] 2 FLR 597 and *Re JK (Adoption: transracial placement)* [1991] 2 FLR 340.[2]

Conclusion

A decision to move a child from a trans-racial placement is indeed very controversial, more controversial than leaving a child in a placement even

---

[2]The author wishes to acknowledge the assistance provided by Yvonne Brown (Yvonne Brown & Co. Solicitors) in researching the reported cases referred to.

where this might effectively be detrimental to the child's emotional well-being in the long term. It is indeed a very complicated and delicate balance of risk. The context of harm should be considered in comparison to other forms of harm: such as the harm suffered as a result of emotional, or sexual or physical abuse; here the attachment argument is rarely used when the impact upon the child's emotional well being is considered harmful to the child. Why then is the attachment argument given such priority when it relates to race? Decisions are made in courts, are not always sufficiently open minded to give full consideration to some of these difficult questions which require careful deliberation. Questions such as the consideration of the socio-political context of the placement, theories of attachment and identity development as well as insight and awareness, and recognition of the detrimental impact upon blacks of direct, indirect and institutional racism.

7 The Evidence of Experts

Judge Roger Connor

This chapter seeks to set out the essential features of the law concerning the evidence of expert witnesses and to describe how this aspect of the law and practice of the courts has developed in relation to proceedings concerning children over the past 30 years or so. At the conclusion of the chapter I shall add some observations of my own about good practice in this field.

The Law

General
Any witness may give evidence of his opinion, that is to say of inferences drawn from facts, rather than the facts themselves. ('He was red in the face and shouting (facts), he was angry (inference).') There is, of course, an intermediate area in which it is difficult to say whether the statement is one of fact or inference. ('He sounded angry.' 'That is my husband's signature.') However, there is a rule within the law of evidence that a witness may not give his opinion on matters which call for the special skill or knowledge of an expert[3] unless, of course, they have that special skill or knowledge, acquired by learning or experience. ('He was red in the face and shouting because he was suffering from a psychiatric disorder.' Evidence that only an expert would be permitted to give.)

For an expert opinion to be admissible in evidence, the facts upon which it is based must be admitted or established by other, admissible evidence[4]. The problems arising from the application of that principle are less acute in civil proceedings, in which hearsay evidence is admissible.

Whilst it has been recognised by the courts at least since the 16th century[5] that it is 'a commendable thing in our law' that the help of those with specialist expertise will be sought if matters arise 'which concern other sciences or faculties,' nevertheless, the courts (particularly the criminal courts) have resisted the introduction of expert evidence in order to determine matters where, 'on the proven facts a judge or jury can form their own conclusions without help ... The fact that an expert witness has impressive scientific qualifications does not by that fact alone make their

---

[3] See *Sherrard* v. *Jacob* [1965] NI 151, at 157,8 per Lord MacDermott
[4] See e.g. *Blagojevic* v. *HM Advocate* 1995 SLT 1189
[5] *Buckley* v. *Rice-Thomas* (1554) 1 Plowd 118

opinion on matters of human nature and behaviour within the limits of normality any more helpful than that of the jurors themselves, but there is a danger that they may think it does'[6].

There is also a body of authority to the effect that evidence of opinion may not be proffered on an ultimate issue, i.e. upon the essential question that the court has to decide[7]. That rule has been abolished and replaced, so far as civil and family proceedings are concerned, by section 3 of the Civil Evidence Act 1972:

1. *Subject to any rules of court . . . where a person is called as a witness in any civil proceedings, his opinion on any relevant matter on which he is qualified to give expert evidence shall be admissible in evidence.*

2. *In this section 'relevant matter' includes an issue in the proceedings in question.*

Civil proceedings concerning children

Resistance by the judges to the introduction of the evidence of experts upon issues thought to be matters requiring only common sense and knowledge of the world formerly extended to family proceedings[8]. In the early 1980s independent social workers made a brief appearance, their disappearance being hastened by a Practice Direction issued in 1983 by the President of the Family Division[9].

The power of the court to maintain control over the use of experts during this period was based upon section 12 of the Administration of Justice Act 1960, which forbids the publication of information relating to certain proceedings (including wardship proceedings and other proceedings concerning children) before a court sitting in private. In addition, the requirement to obtain the leave of the court before a child who is a ward of court could

---

[6]Per Lawton LJ in *R* v. *Turner* [1975] QB 834
[7]See e.g. *North Cheshire and Manchester Brewery Co* v. *Manchester Brewery Co* [1899] AC 83, at 85.
[8]See e.g. *J and Another* v. *C and Others* [1970] AC 668. 'There seem to me to be two completely different cases to be considered. First, where the infant is under some treatment or requires some treatment for some physical, neurological or psychological malady or condition. In such cases medical evidence if accepted must weigh heavily with the court. Secondly, . . . you have the case of a happy and normal infant in no need of medical care and attention for any malady or condition who is sent to a psychiatrist or other medical practitioner for the sole purpose of calling the practitioner to give quite general evidence upon the dangers of taking this, that or the other course in the relevant proceedings. . . . such evidence may be valuable if accepted but it can only be an element to support the general knowledge and experience of the judge in infancy matters . . .' per Lord Upjohn at 726.
[9][1983] FLR 450 and see *Re C (Wardship: Independent Social Worker)* [1985] FLR 56.

be examined for forensic purposes, was extended to all children who are the subject of proceedings[10].

These developments marked a decrease in reluctance to allow expert evidence in proceedings concerning 'normal' children, although it is clear that the judges were concerned about the resulting increases in the cost[11] and length of hearings[12] as well as the need to spare children from distress resulting from a multiplicity of investigations[13].

The position is now governed by the Family Proceedings Rules 1991[14] as follows:

4.18. Expert Evidence: examination of child

1. *No person may, without the leave of the court, cause the child[15] to be medically or psychiatrically examined, or otherwise assessed, for the purpose of the preparation of expert evidence for use in the proceedings.*
2. *An application for leave under paragraph (1) shall, unless the court otherwise directs, be served on all parties to the proceedings and on the guardian ad litem.*
3. *Where the leave of the court has not been given under paragraph (1), no evidence arising out of an examination or assessment to which that paragraph applies may be adduced without the leave of the court.*

4.23. Confidentiality of documents

1. *Notwithstanding any rule of court to the contrary, no document, other than a record of an order, held by the court and relating to proceedings to which this Part applies shall be disclosed, other than to:*
   —a party
   —the legal representative of a party
   —the guardian ad litem

---

[10] *B(M)* v. *B(R)* [1968] 3 All ER 170. 'I think it was unfortunate, though I do not want to be unduly critical, that in this case the paediatrician who was instructed was instructed only by one party, and only had the advantage of hearing that party's views. When similar situations arise in the future, I would strongly urge that parents who are in dispute with each other should at least co-operate in jointly instructing a doctor or paediatrician or psychiatrist in the event of its being thought desirable to obtain an expert opinion', per Wilmer LJ. This is, perhaps, the first statement of this, now well established, proposition. See also *Practice Directions (Costs: Psychiatric Reports)* [1985] FLR 355 and *(Children: Psychiatric Reports)* [1995] FLR 1149.
[11] The rates of remuneration currently allowed to members of the medical profession of consultant status upon the assessment of the costs of publicly funded litigants is in the order of £100 to £150 an hour. If such an expert is required to write a report and to give evidence, the increase in the cost of the case (bearing in mind that it will increase the work to be done by the lawyers) is likely to be in the order of £3,000 to £5,000. Where more than one expert is involved, the resulting increase in cost can be considerable.
[12] See the *Practice Directions (Costs: Psychiatric Reports)* [1985] FLR 355.
[13] See e.g. *Re C (Minors) (Wardship: Medical Evidence)* [1987] 1 FLR 418.
[14] SI 1991/1247.
[15] I.e. the child who is the subject of the proceedings.

—*the Legal Aid Board*[16]
– *a welfare officer*
without leave of the judge or district judge.

2. *Nothing in this rule shall prevent the notification by the court or the proper officer of a direction under section 37(1)*[17] *to the authority concerned.*

3. *Nothing in this rule shall prevent the disclosure of a document prepared by a guardian ad litem for the purpose of:*
—*enabling a person to perform functions required by regulations made under section 41(7)*[18]*:*
—*assisting a guardian ad litem or a reporting officer . . . who is appointed under any enactment to perform his functions.*

The court's leave is, therefore, required before the contents of documents that form part of the evidence filed in the proceedings can be released to an expert, or the expert can examine the child. It will be observed that there is no express prohibition upon the instruction of an expert to prepare a report, provided that the report can be prepared without sight of the filed evidence or an examination of the child. However, a party seeking to by-pass the court's control of expert evidence by such means may well have difficulty obtaining leave to file the report and, in due course, the necessary authority for the recovery of the costs involved if the party in question relies upon public funding[19].

In general, communications between a party to litigation and his lawyer are treated as confidential by the courts. They are subject to what is called, 'legal professional privilege'[20]. However, a majority of the House of Lords has ruled that:

the privilege attaching to reports by third parties prepared for a client, attached only to documents or other written communications prepared with a view to litigation and, moreover, there was no property in the opinion of an expert witness, who could be subpoenaed to give evidence by the other side and could not refuse to answer questions as to his factual findings and opinion. Care proceedings under Pt IV of the 1989 [Children] Act were non-adversarial and investigative proceedings in which the judge was concerned to make a decision which was in the best interests of the child in question. Accordingly, not only was the notion of a fair trial between opposing parties of far less importance in care proceedings than in normal adversarial actions, but care proceedings were so far removed from normal actions that litigation privilege had no place

---

[16] Now the Legal Services Commission.
[17] Of the Children Act 1989.
[18] Of the Children Act 1989.
[19] See e.g. *Re C (Wardship: Independent Social Worker)* [1985] FLR 56.
[20] See *R. v. Derby Magistrates' Court ex parte B* [1995] 4 All ER 526.

in relation to reports obtained by a party thereto which could not have been prepared without the leave of the court to disclose documents already filed or to examine the child[21].

Since the enactment of the Children Act 1989, courts have concentrated upon the management of cases to a much greater extent than previously. In July 1990 (before the Children Act had come into force) Mr Justice Cazalet, a judge of the Family Division[22], gave guidance upon the preparation of reports and the giving of evidence by expert witnesses in cases concerning the welfare of children. This remains the most important statement upon these matters and therefore, it is set out in full:

1. *Expert witnesses are in a privileged position; indeed, only experts are permitted to give an opinion in evidence. Outside the legal field the court itself has no expertise and for that reason frequently has to rely on the evidence of experts.*
2. *Such experts must express only opinions which they genuinely hold and which are not biased in favour of one particular party. Opinions can, of course, differ and indeed quite frequently experts who have expressed their objective and honest opinion will differ, but such differences are usually within a legitimate area of disagreement.*
3. *Experts should not mislead by omissions. They should consider all the material facts in reaching their conclusions and must not omit to consider the material facts which could detract from their concluded opinion.*
4. *If experts look for and report on factors which tend to support a particular proposition or case, their report should still:*
   —provide a straightforward, not a misleading opinion
   —be objective and not omit factors which do not support their opinion
   —be properly researched
5. *If the expert's opinion is not properly researched because he or she considers that insufficient data is available, then the expert must say so and indicate that the opinion is no more than a provisional one.*
6. *In certain circumstances experts may find that they have to give opinions adverse to the party which instructed them. Alternatively if, contrary to the appropriate practice an expert does provide a report which is other than wholly objective, that is one which seeks to 'promote' a particular case, the report must make this clear. However, such an approach should be avoided because it would (a) be an abuse of the position of the expert's proper function and privilege and (b) render the report an argument, not an opinion.*

---

[21] *Re L (A Minor) (Police Investigation: Privilege)* [1997] AC 16.
[22] Note *Re R (a minor) (Expert's Evidence)* [1991] 1 FLR 291.

This guidance was extended by Mr Justice Wall in three cases reported in 1994[23] in which he emphasised the importance of the court exercising control over the evidence to be put before it. These developments were noted with approval by Dame Margaret Booth DBE in her report of July 1996, *Avoiding Delay in Children Act Cases* and a year later, by the Children Act Advisory Committee[24] whose *Handbook of Best Practice in Children Act Cases*[25] contains detailed guidance on a number of subjects, including 'Experts and the Courts.' These important recommendations are summarised below[26].

A child who is *Gillick*[27] competent may decline to consent to a medical or psychiatric assessment and solicitors acting for such a child should make this clear to the child[28]. However, the child should be warned that their decision might be overridden by the court[29]. The child (and, of course, an adult client) should also be warned of the risk that flows from the instruction of an expert, namely that the expert's report, which may contain adverse information, will have to be disclosed to the court and the other parties.[30]

Among the most difficult cases any court has to try are those concerning allegations of sexual abuse of children, often requiring the court to make decisions about the credibility of the child concerned. Where the child has been interviewed and the interview recorded on tape, expert evidence as to the assessment of the child's answers is often of great assistance to a judge:

The judge will also receive expert evidence to explain and interpret the video. This expert evidence will cover such things as the nuances of emotion and behaviour, the gestures and the body movements, the use or non-use of language and its imagery, the vocal inflections and intonations, the pace and pressure of the interview, the child's intellectual and verbal abilities, or lack of them, and any signs or the absence of signs of fantasising[31].

[23] *Re M (Minors) (Care Proceedings: Child's Wishes)* [1994] 1 FLR 749, *Re MD and TD (Minors) (Time Estimates)* [1994] 2 FLR 336 and *Re G (Minors) (Expert Witnesses)* [1994] 2 FLR 291. See also *A Handbook for Expert Witnesses in Children Act Cases, Mr Justice Wall with Iain Hamilton, Family Law, 2000.*
[24] Established in 1991 to monitor the operation of the Children Act 1989 and to comment on issues arising from its implementation but no longer *extant*.
[25] Published in June 1997.
[26] Section 5 of the Handbook.
[27] I.e. a child who has, 'reached an age where she had a sufficient understanding and intelligence to enable her to understand fully what was proposed, that being a question of fact in each case.' *Gillick v. West Norfolk and Wisbech Area Health Authority and Another* [1986] AC 112 HL.
[28] See paragraph M1 of *Guidance to Good Practice for Solicitors Acting for Children* (5th Edition 2000) published by the Solicitors Family Law Association.
[29] *South Glamorgan County Council v. W and B* [1993] 1 FLR 574.
[30] See *R. v. Derby Magistrates' Court ex parte B* [1995] 4 All ER 526.
[31] Per Ward LJ. in *Re N (Child Abuse: Evidence)* [1996] 2 FLR 214.

The criminal courts, however, continue to hold that such evidence is inadmissible because the assessment of the credibility of the child is a 'matter of human nature and behaviour within the limits of normality'[32,33].

Although the credibility of a witness is thought to lie particularly within the expertise of a judge, nevertheless, the modern view of the civil courts is that regulation of expert evidence as to credibility should be as to weight, rather than admissibility. Even where the evidence goes to *the ultimate question*, 'the judge can safely and gratefully rely upon such evidence, while never losing sight of the fact that the final decision is for him'[34]. Thus, it is open to the judge to reject the evidence of an expert, even when that evidence is the only expert evidence on the point, provided, of course, that he can give cogent reasons for doing so[35].

Practice

Section 5 of the *Handbook of Best Practice in Children Act Cases* (see footnote 22 and text related) contains most helpful guidance in relation to expert witnesses. In summary, the advice given was as follows:

- Applications for leave to instruct experts should be considered by each party at the earliest possible stage of the proceedings in order to avoid serial applications by different parties seeking to counter opinions from experts which do not support their case. Such applications are likely to be refused[36].
- Before a court grants such leave it should satisfy itself that the correct field of expertise has been identified, that the expert selected has the appropriate expertise, is available and can provide a report within an appropriate time scale, will be available to attend the hearing, if required and (preferably) is acceptable to all the parties.
- Wherever possible, experts should be instructed jointly by all the parties.
- The court has a positive duty to enquire into the information provided by the parties about an expert and should never make a generalised order for leave to disclose papers to an expert.
- Reports of experts based solely upon a paper exercise are rarely as persuasive as those based upon interviews and assessment as well as the documentation.
- Experts should not be instructed unless they are willing to take part (if necessary) in discussions with other experts in the same field of expertise.

---

[32] Per Lawton LJ in *R* v. *Turner* [1975] QB 834
[33] In *B* v *B* *(Child Abuse: Contact)* [1994] 2 FLR 713 at 731 Wall J said: '... the analysis of interviews with children is a highly specialised skill which should only be undertaken by an expert in the field. The dangers of misinterpretation are manifest ...' This appears to be a proposition unrecognised by the criminal courts.
[34] Per Butler-Sloss LJ. in *Re M and R (Child Abuse: Evidence)* [1996] 2 FLR 214.
[35] See e.g. *Re B (Care: Expert Witnesses)* [1996] 1 FLR 667.
[36] See *H* v. *Cambridgeshire County Council* [1997 1 FCR 569.

- The letter of instruction should:
  (a) Define the context in which the opinion is sought.
  (b) Set out specific questions for the expert to address.
  (c) Identify any relevant issues of fact to enable the expert to give an opinion on each set of competing facts.
  (d) Specify any examination to be permitted.
  (e) List the documents provided to the expert, which should be presented in a sorted bundle and include an agreed chronology and background history.
  (f) Require, as a condition of appointment, that the expert must, in advance of the hearing, hold discussions with other experts appointed in the same field of expertise[37], and produce a statement of agreement and disagreement on the issues by a specific date.
- The letter of instruction should always be disclosed to the other parties who should be invited to contribute to it and to assist in defining the issues, relevant documentation, history and questions to be addressed.
- Any medical records available to some of the doctors in the case should be made available to other experts and to the court.
- Solicitors must ensure that experts instructed by them are kept up to date with developments in the case.
- Any advocate calling an expert witness must ensure that the witness has seen all fresh, relevant material and is aware of new developments.
- The role of the expert is to provide independent assistance to the court by way of objective, unbiased opinion, in relation to matters within his expertise. Expert evidence presented to the court must be, and be seen to be, the independent product of the expert, uninfluenced by the instructing party.
- Experts must comply with the timetable set by the court and give prompt warning if it appears that this may not be possible.
- The expert's report should:
  (a) State the facts or assumptions upon which his opinion is based and not omit to consider material facts which detract from that opinion.
  (b) Make it clear when an aspect of the case is outside his expertise.
  (c) Indicate when an opinion is provisional due to lack of data.
- An expert should notify the court and the parties if he changes his opinion on a material matter.
- If an opinion is based on the research of others, this must be set out clearly and identified in the report.
- An expert should always read any report of a guardian ad litem before giving evidence.

Additional guidance to solicitors acting for children is contained in the *Guidance to Good Practice for Solicitors Acting for Children* published by the

---

[37] NB. Meetings of experts who are **not** in the same field of expertise are, almost invariably, a waste of valuable time.

Solicitors Family Law Association[38] and expert witnesses will find comprehensive advice in Mr Justice Wall's *A Handbook for Expert Witnesses in
Children Act Cases*[39].

Guardians ad litem

Two important propositions emerge from decisions of the Court of Appeal
in cases decided in March 1996[40] and September 1998[41]. A Guardian ad
litem should take care to recognise the limits of his own expertise. In cases
in which he instructs an expert, he will, in effect, become bound by the
opinions of that expert upon matters within the expert's particular sphere of
expertise.

The earlier case[42] concerned an application by a father for a contact order
opposed by the mother upon the basis of an allegation that the father had
sexually abused the child. A central question in the case was the weight to
be attached to 'disclosures' made by the child in a videotaped interview. In
the course of delivering his judgement in the Court of Appeal, Lord Justice
Ward said:

> *... a Guardian ad litem on the Guardian's Panel usually brings his
> experiences as social worker to bear in the discharge of his duties as
> Guardian ad litem. I endorse the passage in the* Manual of Practice
> Guidance for Guardians ad litem and Reporting Officers *(Doh, 1992 see
> References to Chapter 3), which recommends:*
>> The Guardian should not attempt to appear in Court as an expert
>> witness in matters on which he is not competent and credible in the
>> Court's eyes as this can only undermine the child's case. The
>> Guardian is expected to be an expert in general childcare matters, not
>> an expert in specialist areas.
> *There is a further danger in the Guardian ad litem giving evidence as an
> expert. His duties, certainly in specified proceedings, and I see no reason
> why that should not apply when, exceptionally, he acts in private law
> matters[43] as well, are to safeguard the interests of the child in the manner
> described by the rules. His duty is to 'advise the court' on a number of
> matters including what orders should be made in determining the
> applications. It is impossible for him to advise without having come to his
> own conclusion about the harm the child is alleged to have suffered. He*

---

[38] See paragraph M1 of *Guidance to Good Practice for Solicitors Acting for Children* (5th Edition
    2000) published by the Solicitors Family Law Association.
[39] *Family Law*, 2000.
[40] *Re N (Child Abuse: Evidence)* [1996] 2 FLR 214.
[41] *Re G (Adoption Order)* [1999] 1 FLR 400.
[42] *Re N (Child Abuse: Evidence)* [1996] 2 FLR 214.
[43] I.e. proceedings between private individuals, such as disputes between parents as to contact
    or residence as distinct from 'public law' proceedings involving a local authority, e.g. applying
    for a care order.

has to decide in the exercise of his own duty to safeguard the child's interests whether or not he believes the child. Judges cannot complain if he states that belief as the reason for coming to the conclusion and giving the advice he advances. It may be better if his report and his evidence expressly acknowledge that he realises and accepts that this is the court's decision . . . As one reads the rules, it is not without significance to note that under R4.11 (9) the Guardian is able to obtain such professional assistance which he thinks appropriate, which is an indication by itself of the limitations of his own expertise.

The later case[44] concerned an application for an adoption order made by the child's mother and stepfather. The child's father opposed the application and the hearing was adjourned to enable the Guardian ad litem to obtain, 'an overview of the case from a mental health professional.' A consultant child and adolescent psychiatrist was instructed and, at the adjourned hearing, the Guardian (who supported the application) found herself in disagreement with the psychiatrist whom she had instructed (who recommended a residence order). The Guardian could not accept the psychiatrist's opinion that an adoption order would not make the mother feel more secure, nor that the mother would effectively adjust to the level of contact proposed by the Guardian. In his judgement, with which the other members of the Court of Appeal agreed, Lord Justice Thorpe said[45]:

It seems to me that the Guardian was in an extremely difficult position and I have every sympathy for her as a professional of great experience committed to child welfare and protection. But, in my opinion, once it was agreed between the Guardian and [the psychiatrist] that the mother's anxiety was general and pathological, then the Guardian was bound by the opinion of the expert in psychiatric medicine that she had herself instructed. She could of course contend that the psychiatric opinion did not lead to the litigation conclusions recommended by [the psychiatrist]. But it was not, in my opinion, open to her to differ from [the psychiatrist] within the field of psychiatric medicine.

Conclusions

The work of the family judges has now increased in such quantity and complexity that it is almost unthinkable that the trial of a case of any substance concerning children should be embarked upon without the benefit of expert evidence. Even in relatively common disputes between parents, as to where children should live or whether, and with what frequency they should have contact with a non-resident parent[46], it is virtually impossible

---

[44] *Re G (Adoption Order)* [1999] 1 FLR 400.
[45] At p406.
[46] Disputes about contact and the enforcement of contact orders can be among the most difficult cases that a family court has to decide.

to deal with any but the most simple cases without the expertise of a Court Welfare Officer. Virtually all such cases require the court to have regard to the Welfare Checklist[47]. In order to do so it is necessary to ascertain such things as the wishes and feelings of the child, which the judge, very often, cannot do satisfactorily upon the basis of the evidence of the parties themselves. (It is by no means rare for a child to express one wish to one parent and precisely the opposite to the other. To which (if either) of them is the child expressing his true wishes and feelings?)

At the other end of the scale are public law proceedings in which there may be substantial issues about, say, the causation and dating of injuries sustained by a child and the evidence of witnesses from many different fields of expertise may be necessary.

However, the introduction of more expert evidence into these cases has considerably increased their length and the cost to the public purse. It is tempting, on occasions, to consider what might have been done, in material terms, for a family in which the children have been the subject of applications for care orders if the sums spent upon legal costs and disbursements had, instead, been spent upon a much greater level of social work support, perhaps by way of the provision of therapy for the parents or practical assistance with day-to-day care. I strongly suspect that there are many cases in which such a course would have brought greater benefit to the children. Of course, the judges have no power to direct that such a course should be taken but there is a heavy duty upon them to seek to ensure that cases are tried without undue delay, that children are not exposed to unnecessary investigations and that costs payable out of public funds are not wasted.

The keys to achieving these objects are careful case management by judges or magistrates (or their clerks) with the necessary knowledge, experience and expertise, based upon the early and detailed identification of the issues in the case by the parties, with the court's assistance. It is only when it is known which of the assertions made by the applicant are disputed, and the basis of the dispute is identified that the court can decide whether it is necessary for experts to be brought into the case and, if so, to identify the type of expertise required.

The advantages of instructing a single expert in any particular field are manifest, although this can place a heavy burden upon the expert concerned. Although the provisions within the Civil Procedure Rules which empower the court to require the parties to instruct a single joint expert[48] do not extend to proceedings about children, nevertheless, the court ought to have sufficient authority to require this to be done wherever it is appropriate[49]. Courts will particularly strive to avoid inessential investigations, particularly

[47] Children Act 1989, section 1 (3).
[48] Civil Procedure Rules 1998, Part 35.
[49] See the 1994 judgments of Mr Justice Wall and the Children Act Advisory Committee's *Handbook of Best Practice* referred to above.

where they require intimate or psychiatric examinations of the child. Where such examinations are necessary, they should not be duplicated. Particular care should be taken in such cases in the identification of an expert in whom all the parties will have confidence.

The court should not give leave to disclose papers to an expert or for the expert to see the child unless and until it is satisfied that the identified expert has the necessary expertise within the relevant field, that he can complete any necessary investigation and report within a timescale acceptable to the court and that he will be available to attend the hearing of the case, if required. It is far better for the First Hearing for directions to be adjourned for a week of two so that these matters can be resolved, than it is to discover, much later, that the court's timetable has gone awry because of delay in filing reports or that the Final Hearing has to be adjourned because an expert witness is not available to attend.

In cases in which it is necessary to allow more than one expert in a single field of expertise, they should be encouraged to reach agreement between themselves and, where this is not possible, to limit the issues between them.

There are differences of opinion about the practical arrangements for meetings of experts. Where such meetings are necessary, I take the view that the most appropriate person to chair and be responsible for the minutes of such a meeting is the solicitor acting for the Guardian ad litem. It is almost invariably the case that any such solicitor will have considerable experience in cases of this nature. Lawyers' skills of forensic analysis should assist in defining the issues between the experts and a solicitor's administrative expertise should assist in the prompt preparation of a minute acceptable to all parties.

Over the past 30 years we have witnessed substantial changes in the form and content of litigation concerning children and the greatly increased volume of expert evidence is, no doubt, one of the most significant of those changes. It has required the acquisition of a number of new skills on the part of the solicitors, barristers and judges: identifying the particular form of expertise required in a particular case, finding an expert with that expertise[50] and communicating efficiently with the expert, both in terms of conveying to the expert what is required of them and comprehending what the expert has to say when it is expressed in technical language. There can be little doubt that enormous strides have been made in these respects, but there is still a long way to go before the system operates as speedily and efficiently as children, who are the subject of litigation, have a right to expect.

---

[50] As well as having the required expertise, it is also essential that the expert should understand the requirement to approach the matter in a non-adversarial way. In a different field of family law, it was said in December 1994 by Thorpe J. (as he then was) in *B* v. *B* [1995] 2 FCR 813, 'It is a great fallacy for a litigant to think that their interests are well served by experts who take the high ground on their behalf. All that such experts do is to sustain hopes and expectations of outcome which should long ago have been abandoned and which make it much more difficult for the lawyers who are responsible ultimately for negotiation to bring the parties to ground upon which consensus is obtainable.'

8 Assessing the Competence of the Child to Give Instructions: The Solicitor's Role

Sarah Stevens

Introduction

The right of a child to have their wishes and feelings heard in proceedings concerning them and taken into account as appropriate, according to their age and maturity, is recognised internationally[51] and reflected in domestic legislation[52]. This must however be distinguished from the right to express those views directly to the court. This chapter explores the circumstances in which children in civil proceedings in England and Wales may do so.

The Children Act 1989 governs most proceedings in England and Wales relating to the upbringing of children, who are defined as persons under the age of 18 years. No distinction is drawn between the young child and the older adolescent[53]. The child's welfare is paramount in decisions relating to their care or upbringing and the Act contains a 'Welfare Checklist' of factors to assist the court in determining this, the first of which is 'the ascertainable wishes and feelings of the child in the light of his age and understanding'[54]. This does not however mean that the courts will not overrule the wishes of a mature teenager. They have been quite willing to do so, not only where child's choice would be to place them at serious emotional or physical risk[55] but also in situations where the child's view does not accord with current judicial thinking[56].

In all 'specified' proceedings under the Children Act 1989 (here referred to as public law proceedings) the child is automatically a party to the proceedings and is separately represented by the dual appointment of a

---

[51] UN Convention on the Rights of the Child 1989 Article 12, European Convention for the Protection of Human Rights and Fundamental Freedoms 1950, European Convention on the Exercise of Children's Rights 1996.

[52] Children Act 1989, Human Rights Act 1998.

[53] But see the limitations set out in ss9(6) and (7) and s91(10) and (11) as to orders relating to children over 16 in private law proceedings and s31(3) to children over 17 in public law proceedings.

[54] S1 (3) (a).

[55] *Re W (A Minor) (Medical treatment)* [1992] 4 AER 627.

[56] *Re B (Change of Surname)* [1996] 1 FLR 791 where a court refused to allow children aged 16,14 and 12 to change their surname to that of their mother and step-father despite their strongly expressed wishes.

Guardian ad litem and a solicitor. Specified proceedings are those involving a local authority and broadly speaking cover applications for care and supervision orders, emergency protection orders, contact and discharge applications where children are subject to care or emergency protection orders and secure accommodation orders.

At first sight the functions of the Guardian and solicitor appear different but complementary, providing a direct route to the court for the child through his solicitor while ensuring that his welfare interests are articulated through his Guardian. The Guardian investigates all the circumstances of the case, including the child's wishes and feelings and then advises the court as to what is in that child's best interests[57]. The Guardian's recommendations may not fully, or sometimes even partially, reflect the child's wishes. By contrast the solicitor's duty is to represent the client who, irrespective of age or maturity, is the child[58]. However as discussed below, the reality for the majority of children is that the solicitor acts on the instructions of the Guardian rather than the child. Thus although the child's views are reported to the court it is the Guardian's views which are advocated where they differ from those of the child. It is therefore very important for a child whose views do differ from those of his Guardian, that his competence to instruct his solicitor direct be established, thus enabling his views to be fully argued and supported by the challenging of evidence as he directs.

The Law

The duty to determine competence is placed on the solicitor who in addition must consult with the Guardian. In essence the test is:

1. Whether the child is able to give instructions having regard to their understanding.
2. If so whether those instructions conflict with those of the Guardian.
3. Does the child wish to be directly represented?

Unless all three criteria are fulfilled then the solicitor must act in accordance with instructions received from the Guardian[59]. If there is conflict between the views of the Guardian and a competent child then the former must bring this to the attention of the court and seek leave to be separately represented[60]. If the Guardian and solicitor do not agree as to the child's competence the court will decide[61]. Even where they are agreed it is however ultimately for the court to decide whether or not a child is competent[62]. If so the solicitor continues to represent the child while the Guardian will either

[57]Family Proceedings Rules (FPR) 1991 r4 (12).
[58]FPR 1991 r4 (11).
[59]FPR 1991 r4 12(a).
[60]FPR 1991 r4 11(3).
[61]*Re M (Minors) (Care proceedings: child's wishes)* [1994] 1 FLR 749.
[62]*Re CT* [1993] 2 FLR 278.

represent themselves or have leave to instruct a new solicitor. The solicitor must be alert to the possibility that the child may choose to have a new solicitor not associated with the Guardian, in which case the solicitor must then consider, bearing in mind their knowledge of the cases of both the child and the Guardian, whether they face a conflict of interests in continuing to represent the Guardian. If the child is competent then their instructions must be followed even if contrary to their best interests as perceived by the solicitor[63].

There is no essential difference between representing a competent child and an adult. 'It is much more than instructing a solicitor as to their own views. The child enters the arena among other adult parties. They may give evidence and be cross-examined. They will hear other parties, including in this case their parent. They must be able to give instructions on many different matters as the case goes through its stages and to make decisions as the need arises'[64].

The courts have indicated that the decision as to competence should be made early to ensure that all parties have timely representation and late applications for adjournments are avoided[65].

Judicial Guidance

Neither in the Children Act 1989 itself nor in the applicable rules[66], is there any further guidance on how to determine competence. In the early days of the Act the *Gillick* case[67], which considered the capacity of a child under the age of 16 to consent to medical treatment, seemed to provide a test equally applicable to the issue of legal competence. The House of Lords held that 'the parental right yields to the child's right to make their own decisions when they reach a sufficient understanding and intelligence to be capable of making up their mind on the matter requiring decision'. Where therefore even quite young children demonstrated an ability to discuss the issues and potential consequences of different courses of action in the litigation in a reasonably sensible manner solicitors were inclined to accept instructions from them direct.

This was familiar territory for magistrates accustomed under the previous legislation to children being parties and attending court for part or all of the proceedings. Under the Children and Young Persons Act 1969, children (but not their parents) were parties and if over the age of five, had to be brought to court. While most left after a short explanation from the bench as to the purpose of the hearing, older children who wished to remain were often allowed to do so. Unless a guardian had been appointed the solicitor either

---

[63]P4 *Guide to Good Practice For Solicitors Acting for Children*, see References.
[64]*Re H (A Minor) (Role of Official Solicitor)* [1993] 2 FLR 552 FD.
[65]*Re CE* [1995] 1FLR 26.
[66]Much of the detail and procedural guidance is set out in the Family Proceedings Rules 1991 (applicable in the County and High Court) and the Family Proceedings Courts (Children Act 1989).
[67]*Gillick v West Norfolk and Wisbech Area Health Authority* [1986] AC 112.

took his instructions from the child, the child's parents or acted in what he deemed to be the child's best interests. Judges, unless a child was made a ward of court, were rarely involved and although they had discretion to see a child rarely exercised it.

Soon after the implementation of the Children Act 1989, the Court of Appeal determined that it was for the courts to make the ultimate decision as to the child's competence[68]. The higher courts have shown considerable reluctance to allow children to participate directly in the proceedings or even to attend court[69] principally from a desire to protect the child but also perhaps, because it engenders uncomfortable feelings in the judiciary and other parties[70]. While no single reported case offers comprehensive guidance to the solicitor as to how competence is to be assessed, the courts have given some indicators:

- Although understanding ordinarily increases with time, there is no absolute demarcation based on age[71].
- Understanding is not absolute but has to be assessed relative to the issues in the case[72].
- If the child's instructions run counter to what would clearly not be considered by the court, to be in their best interests then they are unlikely to be held competent[73].
- There is a balance between the right of children to participate in their proceedings and the need to protect them from exposure to material, which may be damaging to them[74].
- The child needs to demonstrate independent thought, and maturity, together with clarity and consistency in their instructions[75].
- A child must demonstrate rationality as well as understanding, and this may not be the case where a child is seriously emotionally disturbed[76]. However the fact that a child's instructions may be contradictory or influenced by emotional disturbance may not bar them[77].

It is noteworthy that virtually all the reported cases deal with children of the age of eleven upwards; mostly thirteen to sixteen and by no means all of them uphold the solicitor's views on competence. The underlying sense is one

---

[68] *Re CT* [1993] 2 FLR 278.
[69] s95 CA 1989 permits proceedings to take place in the absence of the child. The Guardian must advise the court as to whether it is in the child's interests to be excused from part of all of the proceedings.
[70] *Re A (Care: Discharge Application by Child)* [1995] 1 FLR 599, FD; *Re W* [1994] *The Times* 13/7/94; Children Act Advisory Committee annual reports 1994 and 1997.
[71] *Re S (A Minor) (Independent Representation)* [1993] 2 FLR CA.
[72] *Re S (A Minor) (Independent Representation)* [1993] 2 FLR CA.
[73] *Re CT* [1993] 2 FLR 278.
[74] *Re A (Care: Discharge Application by Child)* [1993] 2 FLR CA.
[75] *Re SC (A Minor) (Leave to Seek a Residence Order)* [1994] 1 FLR 96.
[76] *Re H (A Minor) (Care Proceedings: Child's Wishes)* [1993] 1 FLR 440.
[77] *Re CT* [1993] 2 FLR 278.

of caution, and of relying on the transmission of the child's wishes and feelings by professional third parties, where there is any doubt about a child's competence. Moreover although magistrates are still more inclined than the higher courts, to accept children as competent and to allow them to attend court, solicitors seem much more cautious and the number of separate representation orders has fallen since the early days of the Act.

In a recent study of eighteen Children Panel solicitors only two found case law useful in this area[78].

Guidance and Training for Solicitors

In general the Guardian appoints the child's solicitor and does so from the Law Society Children Panel. Panel members have a certain level of expertise. They may not join the Panel until they have three years post-qualification experience as a solicitor. They must complete a two day Law Society approved training course and be able to demonstrate both on the (detailed) written application form and in interview by a Children Panel solicitor and guardian that they have sufficient experience of and expertise in this type of work. Considerable additional reading is expected. However few solicitors have any specialist training or experience in child development or communication with children.

While there is considerable emphasis in publications produced by the Law Society and others as to the need to keep the possibility of separate representation under review there is little or no guidance on how to actually measure a child's understanding or translate concepts like maturity into practice. Typical is the following 'maturity can be assessed on the child's ability to understand the nature of the proceedings and to have an appreciation of the possible consequences of the applications before the court both in the long and the short term . . . as the proceedings progress the child will need to understand . . . what the parents and other parties want for the child; what the Guardian and other experts recommend . . . and an outline of the essential law relevant to the proceedings'[79].

Child Development Research

While the pace of development will vary between individual children, research does provide some useful guidelines.

It is now generally accepted that 'there appear to be fundamental psychological differences between the competence of young children aged up to about eleven or twelve, and that of adolescents . . .' and 'it is during early adolescence that young people's thinking becomes more abstract, multi-

---

[78] Feltham, H., *How do Children Panel Solicitors Ascertain the Wishes and Feelings of their Child Clients in Public Law Cases under the Children Act 1989*, see References.
[79] SFLA, *Guide to Good Practice for Solicitors Acting for Children*, see References.

dimensional, self-reflective and self-aware, with a greater use of relative, rather than absolute, concepts'[80].

However of relevance to this debate may be some research into the ability of children in hospital to comprehend and participate in decisions relating to their medical care. 'Many children exceed many adults in, for example, intelligence, ability, prudence, confidence, size, strength and profound experience of certain aspects of life . . .' The researchers concluded that all five year olds should be deemed competent to consent to all medical care[81].

In the same way that sick children, through their first hand experience of illness and the impact of various forms of treatment on them, are able to take a realistic view of prospective treatment so it may be that children who have suffered abusive experiences have a fundamental understanding of those experiences which at least entitles them to have a direct voice in decisions about their future care.

Research with children in public law proceedings suggests that 'many young children are able to differentiate between their ideal wishes and the reality of the options open to them'[82].

What Solicitors do in Practice

When first instructed the solicitor may know little more than the age of the child and the brief information contained in the local authority's application. The court may already have made urgent orders having been satisfied of the need to do so, before a Guardian or solicitor has been appointed. Frequently the first court hearing attended by the solicitor will be within a day or so, and there is little time to see the child or make a considered judgment as to their ability and wish to be separately instructed. Nonetheless it is essential to see children who may be competent, as decisions which determine the course a case takes are very frequently made at the early hearings. These may include orders which determine whether a child remains at home, moves to local authority care or to relatives during the proceedings and how much contact with family members will be allowed. The court will also direct the filing of evidence, which, if any, experts will be appointed, which of these will be expected to see the child, and what the timetable of the proceedings will be.

The writer's starting point is that any child over the age of twelve is likely to be competent and therefore must be seen urgently and before any court hearing, if possible. If not, any orders should be for the shortest practical time to enable the child to be seen, and they should preserve the current position as far as possible. Otherwise the position of a competent child may

---

[80]Taken from a review of the literature by Fortin, J. in *Childrens Rights and the Developing Law*, p 66, see References.
[81]Alderson, P. and Montgomery, J., *Health Care Decisions: Making decisions with Children* [1996] IPPR quoted by Fortin, J. at p64 see References.
[82]Ruegger, M., *Seen and Heard but How Well Informed* (see References) a study of 47 children aged between 8 and 17, at p24.

be compromised. Younger children are less likely to be accepted as competent by a court, therefore any such application on their behalf is unlikely to be successful unless the solicitor has carried out much more extensive enquiries than is likely to be possible at this early stage. However a younger child should also be seen if possible, as their wishes and feelings constitute an important aspect of their representation. Although ultimately the Guardian will give instructions where a child is not competent, the client remains the child and therefore the solicitor must establish the child's views on the full range of short-term as well as long-term issues, discuss them with the Guardian and where they differ see whether there is any way in which the child's wishes can be accommodated.

While age is clearly a factor, it will be a bold solicitor who disregards judicial guidance and seeks to argue that children under the age of eight or even ten are competent; age is only a small part of the equation.

'Understanding' and 'maturity' are value-laden terms meaning different things to different people. In making their assessment the solicitor has to attempt to set aside their own pre-conceptions and prejudices and be able to articulate concrete, professional reasons which will be judicially acceptable.

This means talking to the child, on their own, on several occasions, if possible prior to making an initial assessment, and then keeping the situation under review. It is not uncommon for children who are unable or unwilling initially to express views or demonstrating sufficient understanding, to be able to do so by the Final Hearing.

The Guardian must be consulted, and may well have valuable information from talking to parents and other relatives, teachers, social workers and others, which will help the solicitor. The Guardian's own assessment is also important; they are usually qualified and experienced social workers with proven expertise in working with children, skills that the solicitor is unlikely to have. The courts regard guardians as experts in social work matters and their view will be influential if there is a difference of opinion, which the court has to settle. Accordingly a solicitor will need a well-reasoned argument to prevail over the Guardian's view. Others whom they may consider consulting include parents, teachers and others with good knowledge of the child and those with expertise in the field, for example, child psychiatrists, psychologists and the like. However the delay in obtaining expert opinions is likely to rule this out unless the expert is already treating the child or has been instructed in the case. The solicitor also needs to keep in mind that a competent child is owed the same duty of confidentiality as any other client and their permission should therefore be sought before approaching anyone other than the Guardian.

As part of the process the solicitor will need to discuss the reasons for the application, outline the evidence and the other parties' views, explain the legal position, and talk through the options with the child. The way in which the child responds to this frequently determines the twin issues of whether the child has sufficient understanding and wishes to be directly involved in all or any of the issues with which the court is concerned. A child has the same right as any other client to decline to be involved and that is the choice that many children, with torn loyalties and confused feelings, make. They may agree with the Guardian's views, but prefer them to come from the Guardian, or they may simply prefer the adults or the judge to make the decisions. If there is no difference with the Guardian then the question of separate representation does not arise.

However where children of about ten upwards are able to express a clear and apparently reasoned view, to understand the solicitor's explanations and the implications of their chosen course of action, then the solicitor must seriously consider separate representation. At that stage they also need to discuss with the child what it will mean in practice: for example, going through the evidence in detail, putting the child's statement into court, attending the hearing, seeing and hearing their parents and others being cross-examined and possibly giving oral evidence and being challenged on it themselves. The child also needs to understand that the judge may well *not* order what they want.

The child may not wish to be involved to that extent. Some practical steps can be taken to reduce the potential distress of, for example, attending court by ensuring that they do not have to wait in the same area as adults whom they do not wish to see, or by giving evidence by video-link or behind a screen. However direct representation will involve the child much more intensively, and potentially place them under greater pressure, than will consultation with representation through the Guardian. The solicitor must be alert to this, establish precisely what level of involvement the child wants and devise imaginative ways to achieve this.

Children may for example want to see some but not all of the written or oral evidence, to see the court, to see or talk directly to the judge or magistrates who will make the decisions, to make a written statement setting out their views, to hear their solicitor make the submissions on their behalf or to hear the decision. With the co-operation of the court these can all be achieved without the child feeling compelled either to take a full role in the proceedings or none at all.

Moreover these proceedings are a dynamic process. As evidence is gathered and discussed, parties' perceptions frequently change, actions are modified, and mutually acceptable outcomes may be negotiated. While it may be possible to make a decision as to *competence* at an early stage it is frequently not clear whether the child's view will ultimately be different from that of the Guardian, or whether they will wish to be separately represented, which militates against the early decision recommended by the courts.

Some Common Dilemmas for the Solicitor

- How much understanding is required? Is it sufficient for a child to understand the broad issues and evidence, explained in simple language by the solicitor or must they be able to understand, and even read, the evidence?

- To what extent is intelligence a factor? For example, should a learning-disabled child be automatically deemed incompetent, even if they are able to express a view which is consonant with the issues?
- Many children in public law proceedings will have been profoundly affected by the experiences which have led to the proceedings. What allowance should be made for this in the assessment of the child's emotional maturity? Should the comparison be with a similar (i.e. abused) child or with an 'average' non-abused child?
- Does a child showing excessive or little emotion in talking to the solicitor indicate a lack of emotional maturity, or is it an entirely understandable response to the situation in which they find themselves? What about children diagnosed as emotionally or behaviourally disturbed?
- How important is it that the child is able to articulate a point of view, to discuss and consider alternative points of view? This may rule out the many children who have a very clear idea of what they want but find it difficult to put their reasoning into words, and those who, having made their views plain, do not wish to discuss the evidence or alternatives further. Neither of these situations necessarily means that they do not understand the choices they are making or that they would not wish to have those views argued on their behalf.
- What about consistency of instructions? Adults may also find it difficult to be consistent yet are not debarred from direct representation.
- How important is it that the child's instructions can be implemented in practice, for example, where they wish to return home but their parents are not asking for this?
- To what extent are they influenced by others: and if that influence is perceived as coming from their parents or other significant family members how should that be evaluated given that influencing one's child is seen as an essential component of good parenting?
- Should the potential risks of the child's choice affect this decision: or is that a factor for the court on the application itself?
- Should the solicitor consider the impact upon the child of the child's participation in the proceedings? What effect will it have on their view of the proceedings and of the decisions, which are made to promote their long-term well-being, if they are not allowed to participate? Alternatively, will the impact of full participation in itself have a detrimental effect? This can cause particular difficulties when the evidence filed includes not only the factual evidence leading to the proceedings, which will almost always be known to the child, but assessments of parents or carers which may well contain very personal and revealing information of which the child may not be aware[83].
- Should different criteria apply depending on the nature of the application? If so, should it depend on the significance of the application for the child's

---

[83]But see *Re B (A Minor)* [1993] 1 FLR 191 which confirmed that directions may be sought from the court as to disclosure.

life or the complexity of the decision to be made? Most solicitors would take direct instructions from a child facing an application for secure accommodation who, although usually aged 13 upwards, would probably fail most of the judicial guidance set out above. However the same child may well not be deemed competent in a care application which will in practical terms determine where they live and who has ultimate authority over them. What about more straightforward issues like contact?

- Particular difficulties arise with applications made within proceedings. For example care applications often also involve applications for contact or for a child to be examined by an expert. In the latter case a child may refuse if they are of sufficient understanding to make an informed decision[84]. In reality it is impossible for a solicitor to accept direct instructions from the child on some issues, and the Guardian on others, in the same proceedings.

- What will the impact on the child be, if the court disagrees with the solicitors view that the child is competent?

Research into Solicitors' Practice

There has been some direct research with solicitors on the specific issue of competence. For example, in 1994 Sawyer interviewed 18 members of the Children Panel of varying experience as to their own practice, and seeking their responses to questions based on three vignettes[85].

Most of the solicitors were clear that it is their responsibility to make the decision. Although they were glad to have the guidance of the Guardian they may not accept their advice. They did not otherwise rely on professional advice and 'had comparatively little regard for the opinions of experts on a child's competence within the proceedings'.

They applied 'their own pragmatic considerations to the particular case based on what they considered to be the best way of achieving the appropriate outcome for the case in hand'.

Given the frequently drawn analogy between legal and *Gillick* competence, they were asked whether they considered the two to be the same. Ten felt that legal competence was not necessarily the same as *Gillick* competence, with only eight seeing the test as being the same (seven) or nearly so (one):

> ... *you cannot assume a child is competent to look at the long-term ramifications ... A child aged ten is probably competent over a contact application but not medical treatment.*

But the converse may also be true:

---

[84]S38(6) but note the understanding is higher than that required to instruct a solicitor and the child's refusal may be overruled by the court—*Re H (A Minor) (Care Proceedings)* [1993] 1 FLR 440.
[85]Sawyer, *The Rise and Fall of the Third Party*, see References.

Gillick *includes giving instructions but I would question whether giving instructions includes* Gillick *competence. It depends on the issue.*

Specifically asked whether they had an age at which they would presume competence in the average child, eleven solicitors chose ages fairly evenly across the range ten to fifteen (remaining clear that age was only a presumption displaceable by other factors) while seven found the question too simplistic:

> *You can have an incompetent teenager. Maybe 10 or 11. It could be 9 or 8 . . .*

Maturity and the ability to articulate feelings were commonly cited but without analysis of what those concepts mean or how they may be weighted against children of a different culture or class:

> *. . . if their reasons are sound and they are able to express them properly: this is not an intelligence test. . .*
>
> *. . . difficult to deal with less intelligent and articulate clients.*

They readily accepted that their adult clients may well fail a similar test of competence but would continue to act for them, making decisions in what they considered their clients best interests, if necessary.

They also saw little incongruity in the same child being competent in criminal but not in civil proceedings:

> *It is different saying a child is responsible because they did something which they know is wrong and where you are responsible for dealing with the future. It's a very big decision, for a child to feel responsible for bad news.*

However there was also a widely held view of the need to empower children by representing them direct, and this was not linked to the rationality of their views or the likely outcome:

> *. . . the general criteria are age, not intelligence but maturity, how the child feels within the proceedings. If they feel powerless and at a loss I would represent them however unreasonable their views, the guardian would put forward a rational view . . .*

The need for separate representation was most readily accepted in secure accommodation applications, perhaps because this was seen as analogous to imprisonment and therefore natural justice required that the child had a voice.

Concern over the burden on the child or the impact on the family as a whole was voiced only in relation to private law proceedings:

In public law a child needs to know what is being said about them if they are old enough. In private law things are said which you don't want them to know, especially about their parents.

What the survey revealed was that in reaching their decisions solicitors relied heavily on their own 'feel' for the child's maturity, the benefit or disadvantage to that child of being involved in this way in the proceedings and their own beliefs as to the right of children to be so represented. While there were varying attitudes, value judgments and unquestioned influences affecting their practice, the impression given was that this was an important aspect of representing children.

Research with Children and Guardians ad litem

This presents a rather different picture.

Studies have repeatedly shown that solicitors do not see much of their child clients, introductory visits almost always take place with the Guardian present and there may be no separate visits at all. Thus in *Out of Hearing*, a 1996 study by Masson and Oakley of 20 children aged nine to sixteen, two solicitors did not see their child client at all, two others for ten minutes or less, six children were seen once or twice and only two on five or more occasions. Moreover half the children only saw their solicitor with their Guardian[86].

While solicitors cited the Guardian's greater skill in communicating with the children, and the lack of purpose in building a relationship where they do not expect to be taking separate instructions many of the children were not happy with their limited involvement:

> *I've only seen her once or twice . . . [my carer] did most of the explaining . . . She didn't really come often which I think she should have done. I would have told her why I run off and all that.*

Some, with the exception of the children who attended court, were confused as to the solicitor's role, and its relationship to that of the Guardian.

None of the children in this study had seen the full evidence and many had seen none of it, including the full Guardian's report. Solicitors generally left discussion of this to the Guardian although a few discussed some aspects of it to clarify points for the hearing, including whether there was disagreement with the Guardian. By this time however, half of the solicitors had effectively disengaged from the child and were dependent on the Guardians to tell them if there was a difference of view.

In Ruegger's study, while all the children were aware that the Guardian would report their wishes and feelings to the court a significant number were

---

[86]See also a study by Clarke in 1995, see References. Of 28 children only one third were seen by their solicitor, and half of those who were not were 8 years or older.

unaware that they had also to make a recommendation which may not reflect these. While clear about the position taken by other parties, many remained unaware of that adopted by the Guardian. Without this the child cannot decide whether they would want to have a different view argued on their behalf and the solicitor is unable to carry out his role in determining whether an application for separate representation should be made. As Ruegger says 'this raises questions about the role of the child's solicitor'[87].

The Impact of Separate Representation on the Relationship between Solicitor and Guardian

The very nature of this work, involving small specialist pools of Guardians ad litem and solicitors, means that the same professionals will tend to work together regularly. From the outset the professional relationship between them has been seen as significantly different from the general relationship between solicitor and client. 'The ingredients are partnership, collaboration, communication and consultation'[88]. The child should form part of a three-way relationship, unless and until there is a separation. However solicitors generally report being led by the Guardian in how they operate professionally, being for example more or less pro-active according to the preferences of the particular Guardian[89]. This seems also to apply to the decision as to competence, both consciously and perhaps unconsciously. While there are good professional reasons for placing weight on the views of the Guardians, they also exercise considerable patronage through their ability to appoint children's solicitors. The loss of a good working relationship may therefore impact profoundly on an individual solicitor's ability to continue in their chosen specialism.

Similarly the nature of the Guardian's individual and independent role, without the support of a management structure or formal peer-group network means that many rely heavily on the solicitor for case discussion and help with the formulation of recommendations, as well as more practical assistance with, for example, experts, and handling the paperwork.

Sawyer explored the dynamics of this situation in a further study[90]. Revealingly, separate representation was a rare occurrence and one in which some of both Guardians and solicitors had no experience. While the solicitors were clear that the decision was for them, albeit with considerable input from the Guardian, the latter were less clear that it was for the solicitor. Both would expect to reach agreement. Whether or not they did they would expect to continue working closely together. Thus a solicitor commented:

---

[87] Ruegger p19 Seen and Heard, see References.
[88] *The Child as Client*, King and Young p17, see References.
[89] Sawyer, *The Rise and Fall of the Third Party*, see References.
[90] Sawyer, *Rules, Roles and Relationships*, see References.

> *I would still expect . . . the Guardian to inform me of new information that they had found . . . which I would need to discuss with my client.*

. . . and a Guardian:

> *I would hope there would continue to be a good exchange of views so that they were able to tell me what the child was thinking*[91].

This reflects the judicially approved non-adversarial approach to children's cases[92] and promotes the possibility of agreement. It also enables the impact of the split on the professionals to be minimised although it sidelines the question of the confidentiality owed to the child. In contrast if the Guardian also had their own solicitor the child's solicitor would not expect the same direct contact without that solicitors' express agreement because it would breach the solicitor's professional ethics.

While the possibility of a split may be identified at an early stage Guardian and solicitor would generally try to continue to work together for as long as possible, in part to enable the Guardian to try and persuade the child to their point of view as one solicitor put it *'being very sensible from the social work point of view . . . I think the outcomes of the cases where they succeed . . . are much better'* but also to modify that of the Guardian. As another solicitor commented:

> *. . . increasingly the way that guardians are using the [1989] Act is that they really dislike getting separated from teenage children . . . they will tend to go along with what the child wants even if it's not . . . what the guardian thinks is brilliant*[93].

A significantly different understanding of the solicitor's role was revealed in comments about the extent to which the solicitor should attempt to persuade the child to the Guardian's view of their best interests.

Most solicitors said they would advise the child, including an assessment of the likely outcome of opposition to the Guardian's view both in terms of the child's welfare and the court proceedings but would not pressurise them. They were generally uncomfortable with the idea that they would press their *own* views of the child's best interests on them and if the child's views remained the same they would represent them unequivocally in court.

By contrast, all the Guardians' responses showed that they saw the solicitor in as much of a welfare role as a legal one. They expected them to form a view as to what was in the child's best interests (which by implication should be the same as the Guardians) and do their utmost to persuade a child holding an unwise view to change their mind. Although only one went

[91] Sawyer *Rules, Roles and Relationships*, see References, pp 92 and 93.
[92] *Oxfordshire County Council* v *M 2* [1994] AER 269.
[93] Sawyer, *Rules, Roles and Relationships*, see References, p99.

so far as to suggest that if unsuccessful the solicitor should decline to represent the child, others had ambivalent views on solicitors continuing to do so:

> *I would not expect to see any responsible lawyer doing that.*

Some suggested a lesser standard of representation would be appropriate:

> *I would think that the solicitor would only do it half-heartedly in order to put it across.*

Some took comfort from the fact that having chosen the solicitor in the first place the Guardian retains some influence by proxy. It was not uncommon for Guardians to consider not instructing that solicitor again and some were clear that they would not, the solicitor's actions being seen as:

> *. . . immoral and improper . . . and that the solicitor would be insufficiently devoted to the cause of child welfare*[94].

While other Guardians were equally clear that if the child did not take their solicitor's 'strong advice' then the solicitor had a duty to represent the child on their instructions, nevertheless this does underline the risk to the solicitor who does not act in accordance with the views of each individual Guardian.

The number of children and Guardians who are actually separately represented is very small indeed.

In Masson and Oakley's study, notwithstanding the ages of the children and the nature of the applications, including four for secure accommodation orders, none of the children were separately represented and most of the solicitors could only recall one or two cases each when this occurred. All were clear that this would alter the relationship between themselves, the Guardian and the child. Masson and Oakley were unequivocal in their conclusion that:

> *The solicitor's way of working appeared to avoid the possibility of conflict arising or becoming apparent. They spent little time with the young person alone . . . ensuring [they] were properly informed . . . and had confidence in them. They did not generally spend time going through the guardian's report, and some only saw the child early in the investigations before the guardian's position had become clear . . . Where conflict did arise . . . solicitors advised against opposing the applications on the basis that compliance would be viewed positively . . .*[95].

Similarly in Ruegger's study no child was separately represented. She questioned whether 'some guardians . . . may be implicitly making decisions

[94]Sawyer, *Rules, Roles and Relationships*, see References, p108.
[95]Sawyer, *Rules, Roles and Relationships*, p 77–78, see References.

about whether children are old enough to give their own instructions without explicitly stating this'[96].

Clearly there are complex causes for the small numbers of separately represented children. Some arise elsewhere, for example in restrictive judicial guidance or in the way in which Guardians strive to mediate and negotiate mutually acceptable outcomes[97]. However the suspicion arises that part of the answer lies in the nature of the relationship between Guardians and panel solicitors, with its overt emphasis on co-working in a non-adversarial manner to *secure the best interests of the child* and the covert patronage exercised over solicitors by the Guardians' unfettered powers of appointment.

Party Status: Private and Public Law Proceedings Compared

In private law proceedings a child is not automatically a party and will need the leave of the court if they are to make their own application or intervene in proceedings between their parents. Application is to the High Court[98] and is a two-stage process. Again the solicitor must determine if 'the minor is able, having regard to their understanding, to give instructions in relation to the proceedings'[99] and so satisfy the court[100]. However the child will also need to satisfy the court that they have a good arguable case and that it is in their best interests to be a party. The courts have stressed that giving leave to child applicants should be viewed cautiously and reserved for matters of importance[101].

The task for a child in private law proceedings is a heavy one. There is no professional or independent support automatically available for them, compared to public law proceedings where a guardian remains in the case where a child is deemed competent. If they have the support of one of the parties, or other adults, the court may well feel either that they are not acting independently in making their application or that there is no need for them to be joined as parties as others will articulate their position for them.

If the court feels that the child should be separately represented but is not competent to instruct a solicitor it may invite the Official Solicitor to represent the child. If the Official Solicitor agrees, they will act in a Guardian role transmitting the child's wishes and feelings, making a recommendation as to best interests and instructing an advocate. Representation may be sought for any child through the Official Solicitor but they will need to be satisfied that the involvement of a court welfare officer will not suffice.

---

[96] Ruegger, *Seen and Heard, but How Well Informed*, see References, p18–19.
[97] See for example the discussion in Clark and Sinclair, *The Child in Focus*, Chapter 6, see References.
[98] Presidents Practice Direction [1993] 1 All ER 820.
[99] FPR 1991 r9.2A.
[100] *Re CT* [1993] 2 FLR.
[101] *Re C (A Minor) (Leave to Seek s8 orders)* [1994] 1 FLR 26.

Without a judicial request the Official Solicitor will act only in very unusual circumstances[102].

Nonetheless the duty remains to ensure that the child's wishes and feelings are heard. Without direct involvement by the child however, this is left to the disputing parties and, where appointed, to the Court Welfare Officer. Unlike a Guardian their role is not to represent the child. Unless they detect child protection issues substantial enough to warrant investigation by the local authority, their main focus is likely to be on mediation and promoting agreement between the adult parties. The *National Standards for Probation Service Family Court Welfare Work* (Home Office, 1994), state that 'all children should be seen by the Court Welfare Officer unless there are strong grounds for not doing so' but there is no absolute obligation to do so. Recent research indicated that 42 per cent of respondents always, and 47 per cent of respondents mostly saw children for the preparation of welfare reports. Of such children 87 per cent were seen separately from their parents. However the views of the Court Welfare Officers as to the weight to be placed on children's views varied considerably[103].

The result is that children, and their views, are substantially unrepresented in any meaningful sense in private law proceedings. Section 64 of the Family Law Act 1996 makes provision for representation of children to be extended to private law proceedings but has not yet been implemented and is under review. It seems unlikely to be implemented in its present form.

Interestingly, many of the solicitors surveyed in Sawyer's research[104] had become concerned about the impact on children of their direct involvement in private law proceedings, had become more cautious as a result and intimated that they would be slower to find a child in private law proceedings competent:

> *I believed my job was to give children a voice and fight the adults who deny children a voice. But in the course of practice I have become very aware of the damaging effects of contentious proceedings on children.*

However what the test might be remained unclear and no-one suggested this justified a higher age for a presumption of competence in these proceedings.

Conclusion

Underlying the debate about the child's competence to participate directly in decision making are the conflicting concepts of the child's right to autonomy, including the right to make mistakes, as against their need for protection, to enable them to reach maturity without impairing their ability to lead a fulfilling adult life. In the judicial context however, what is at stake

---

[102] See Practice Note issued by the Official Solicitor at [1999] 1 FLR 310.
[103] Hester *et al.*, 1997, cited in Day, Sclater and Piper, *Undercurrents of Divorce*, at p 84, see References.
[104] Sawyer, *The Rise and Fall of the Third Party*, see References.

is not the right of a child to make decisions but merely to have their point of view advocated on equal terms with those other parties who have an interest in them. Decision-making remains the function of the court.

Children often articulate concrete and practical wishes: to live with a named person, see or stay over with named people, attend a particular school, take part in activities etc. They may not draw the same conclusions from their experiences as do the adults, whether professional or family. They are children and approach their experiences in a child-like way. Their views are not however necessarily childish or less worthy of respect and consideration than those of the adult participants. Plainly children feel excluded from the judicial process[105] and the challenge is to find ways of engaging them while avoiding further harm.

While it may be possible to 'grasp the nettle of the factors to be taken into account in assessing competence and their weight against each other[106], notwithstanding the palpable difficulties as demonstrated by current practice, it is likely that the professionals, solicitors, Guardians and courts, will continue to implement them very differently in practice as a result of their individual views of the autonomy versus welfare debate.

To achieve consistency it may be preferable to fix an age at which there would be a presumption not of competence but simply of participation in the proceedings *to the extent that the child desired.* This would include the right displaceable only in exceptional circumstances to see all the evidence and attend court. It would seem reasonable to adopt an age of twelve, in line with research and following the pattern of legislation elsewhere[107]. Consideration should also be given to involving younger children rather more, in particular by making them more aware of the Guardian or court welfare officer's recommendations and the reasons for them. If the child wishes, meeting with the judge or magistrates who will be hearing their case, and, afterwards, being told the reasons behind the judicial decision.

To the argument that the court arena is inherently harmful to children it might be countered that the process itself needs to be modified. A shift in the way evidence is presented, both in written form and in court, so as to make the proceedings more suitable for children's participation, by encouraging shorter, clearer evidence more firmly rooted in the essential issues for decision, and a less adversarial stance would benefit all parties. Most importantly it would give real meaning to the objective underlying both international and domestic legislation of giving children a real voice in proceedings concerning them.

---

[105] Masson and Oakley, *Out of Hearing*, pp 104, 114, 116, see References.
[106] Sawyer, *The Rise and Fall of the Third Party*, see References.
[107] See for example the Children (Scotland) Act 1995 s6 under which there is a presumption that a child of 12 years or more is of sufficient age and maturity to form a view on major decisions.

9 From Guardian ad litem to Children's Guardian: New Opportunities?

Vivienne Reed

Introduction

This chapter explores the likely impact of changes in the management and organisation of the work of Guardians ad litem who, since April 2001, have become officers of CAFCASS. Guardians, most of whom have had many years experience, have come into the new service with a background of working as independent practitioners. The new organisational structure requires that they move from an independent position, to one of account-ability to a national agency. The processes that may assist with this transformation, together with some of the advantages for both Guardians and their child clients, are discussed. I have considered how some of the established, and tried and trusted, tools, employed to ensure the professional development of practitioners, can be adapted to sit comfortably within the new organisation, for example mentoring and coaching. Through discussion and case studies, examples of some of the more complex aspects of the work undertaken by Guardians are illustrated. In each of the cases discussed, the Guardian has considered that, in order to do their job properly, they needed to exceed the boundaries of their role. Under previous legislation Guardians had to deal with such conflict without the support of a line manager. This chapter explores the lack of management intervention that operated when the Guardian service was under the administration of the local authority, and compares this experience with the management arrangements that are likely to prevail under CAFCASS.

Changing Culture

The new service, launched in April 2001 under the legislative framework contained in the Criminal Justices and Court Services Act, brings together the Court Welfare Officers, Guardians and those staff from the Official Solicitors Department that were responsible for public and private law cases involving children. CAFCASS is attached to the Lord Chancellors Depart-ment but has agency status, with responsibility being to a Board[108]. Responsibility for accountability is delegated to managers, who overview the

---

[108] For a full discussion on this see *Seen and Heard* Volume 10. Issue 3 (2000).

cases of individual practitioners within a local team, but without directing professional practice. This is in stark contrast to the statutory instruments in the original legislation of the Children Act 1989, found in volume seven of *The Children Act Guidance and Regulations* (Department of Health, 1991), which stressed that Guardians were not accountable to panel managers for their practice.

Guardians ad litem were unique amongst social services personnel in that they were personally accountable to the courts for the work they carried out, and they were not part of a line managed structure. Guardians were not fettered in their independent investigation of a child's circumstances; the extent to which they extended their inquiries was a matter for each individual practitioner. This freedom was strengthened by the 'Cornwall'[109] judgement of 1992 when an individual Guardian successfully sought judicial review of a local authority's decision to set a limit on the amount of hours they worked on specified proceedings. The Cornwall judgement does not apply to CAFCASS. Although individual practitioners own their recommendation and are named on the order of appointment from the court, it is CAFCASS that is accountable for professional practice and resources. Court Welfare Officers, on the other hand, have traditionally been part of a line managed service operated by the Probation Service. The merging of the three cultures of the Court Welfare, Official Solicitor and the Guardian services will need skilled managers who will be able to harness the strengths of the three services. There is a need to look at lessons learnt by other organisations, for example *International Business Machines* (IBM), who lost their position as a leading computer provider because they were not innovative when they changed their structure (Fitts, 1998). The company used the traditional linear or hierarchical models of management and tried to emulate the past, to the detriment of the organisation.

This is not to advocate that the past is forgotten. The Court Welfare service, the Guardian service, and the children's department within the Official Solicitor's office, were *not* ailing, nor did they need radical change to survive. Nevertheless CAFCASS should attempt to create something new, rather than copy any of the old management styles of the previous services. My own view is that CAFCASS should look for organic growth, whereby practitioners and managers work together to identify the way the service can best meet the needs of children and their families. By keeping this key aim in mind, disparate groups can work together in a common aim of developing CAFCASS and through this process, issues arising from cases will be brought to the attention of colleagues and managers. Evidence collected can be fed back to the providers of local services, and to CAFCASS itself, if it is felt that children are being disadvantaged in any way. Practitioners now have the advantage of discussing individual cases with designated people within CAFCASS, who will take overall responsibility for the quality of the service and the individuals within it.

---

[109] *R* v *Cornwall County Council x Parte G* [1992].

A Team Culture

The formation of professional teams that mix practitioners from different backgrounds brings with it a challenge for the management of this new service. Managers would do well to develop a culture of interdependence among the merging practitioners whereby they will feel supported, not threatened, by management and new colleagues alike. The merge should clarify practice issues, giving opportunities for common problems to be aired and correlated by managers. The fact that the practitioners have the generic title of CAFCASS officer is likely to facilitate the shift in culture from independence to interdependence, because personnel will be seen as representing CAFCASS, an organisation that provides varied and different services for children and families.

To achieve cohesive teams, clear opportunities exist for convergence training in both public and private law so that practitioners can learn new skills from each other. Both mentoring and coaching are management tools that have been shown to be effective in transferring skills from one person to another (Pedlar *et al.* 1991). This is not training; this is learning. Those that recommended structures for CAFCASS say they want a learning organisation. In my view learning from each other comes from mentoring and coaching.

Whilst managing the Hertfordshire Guardian ad litem service, I undertook a small scale study on the effectiveness of mentoring in which mentoring was compared with coaching. The findings suggest that the mentoring relationship was successful, in part because the mentor and mentoree were seen as equal by the organisation. The 'report back' element to management was on the practice areas that were covered, rather than the quality of the practice demonstrated by the mentoree. The success was affected by preparation for the mentoring relationship and in particular on the emphasis on equality within this relationship. Both mentor and mentoree learned a great deal about each other's skills, and the mentoree was able to transfer those skills to another culture, those receiving mentoring being newly appointed members of the panel.

The coaching relationships were more problematic. The persons being coached had to reach targets that had been set with a view to improving their practice. However, the coach, because of the legislative framework, could not be the line manager and had to be a peer, either from within the panel or from an external consultant. Peers felt uncomfortable in reporting back to management when making judgements about their colleague's practice. The findings suggest that, to ensure effectiveness, a coaching relationship needs to have line management involvement, with continual review of practice by the line manager. Although this may be learning 'by control', in my view, it is nevertheless sometimes necessary to achieve a high quality output. An organisation can be effective if it has the management structure to facilitate both models of learning to assist staff in their professional development.

It would be an advantage to the organisation if peer group mentoring could be implemented sooner rather than later for managers, administrators and practitioners in CAFCASS. Mentoring can help people cope with change and can assist in preventing the understandable tendency for workers to re-group into their former 'safe' groupings. Peer group mentoring can be effective in a managed service because the 'report back' element is not required, leaving the mentoring pair free to explore each others' working practices, and to discuss personal responses to change. The ideal would be to have acceptance from the Board for a mentoring progamme to facilitate the transformation from initial suspicion, to acceptance, and to respect for each other. The ultimate goal for CAFCASS is to provide a workforce which will deliver a child centered and consistent service to children, families and the courts. This is not to say that practitioners will not have different views about aspects of child care practice, and come to it from different perspectives. This should be encouraged as it can positively influence practice, provided the focus remains on the interest of children, the service recipients. In fact it is likely that practitioners will have a better opportunity to effect change if they have the backing of a large and influential organisation as a powerful lobby.

Independence versus Interdependence

In my experience of combining the two roles of Panel Manager and Guardian, I have been aware of the tensions that dual accountability to both the court and to the Panel can bring. As a manager I have occasionally found that a Guardian has not met the performance indicator or the required standards and yet, case after case, the appraisal reports from the courts have been glowing with praise. The practitioner has felt baffled by criticism as their target and benchmark of quality has been these feedback forms from the court. From one year to the next they have either 'gone it alone', or they have attended support groups that have not challenged their practice, or perhaps they have chosen not to hear the challenge.

The Guardian service measured the quality of Panels by reference to *National Standards* (Department of Health, 1995). Individual Panels in addition established performance indicators to measure the competence of Guardians. As Guardians had little opportunity to discuss the standards as a team, they put their own interpretation on them. In essence, individuals did not have the chance to digest these standards nor apply them to their own performance.

Guardians have traditionally protected their independence fiercely, especially over the issue of appraisal, and they advocated the need for independent appraisers. In the southern region of the country, Panel management colleagues facilitated an independent panel of appraisers and worked alongside them to interpret the performance indicators. The appraisers themselves set up their own support group to interpret the standards consistently. This enabled them to provide an appraisal scheme that was of a high quality, and provides a good example of how a team approach can be effective in service delivery.

The challenge for CAFCASS team managers is to harness the positive experiences from groups such as the independent appraisers in the quest to develop teams that are motivated to reach the same aims and goals in delivering a service.

Managing Conflicts of Role

Contained within the *National Standards* were performance indicators that clarified the boundaries of the role of the Guardian ad litem. On occasion Guardians have taken the decision to exceed this role, or would have wished to do so, to enable them to assist and inform the court fully about the current and future welfare of the child. Often they have had to be pro-active to prevent delay and in doing so have blurred the boundaries of their role. They have had to balance the risk of significant harm with the future welfare of a child, and have sometimes tipped the scales in favour of relatives assuming care of the child, as opposed to entry into the public care system. In these situations the Guardians have at times, for example when faced with local authorities' refusal to consider assessments of potential carers, taken on some of the work normally undertaken by social work staff in order to provide the court with full information as to the circumstances of the child.

Guardians used the court rules (Rule 11), set out in the statutory instrument that governed the powers and duties of the Guardians ad litem under the 1989 Children Act, to bring matters of conflict and complexity back to the court. Directions hearings were used by Guardians to highlight problems that existed between them and the other parties, for example, where they felt that the local authority was not keeping the child's welfare paramount. The court in turn would sometimes instruct, or sanction, the Guardian to undertake a particular activity, if such action would be likely to minimise delay or provide the court with relevant information.

Prior to the launch of CAFCASS, the Guardian had no option but to use the court as a medium for resolving complex issues. There was no *right* to discuss the case with others. Guardians' independence made it impossible to call on any other power to assist them in resolving conflict, or in asking the local authority to review their thinking in those situations where informal overtures failed to bring about the desired response. Panel Managers were often marginalised by the local authority as guidance on their role within the local authority made it clear that the Panel Manager should be 'arms length' from the services provided to children and families. Consequently managers of the Guardian service were not included in child care policy groups, nor did they have membership of the Area Child Protection Committee (ACPC). It is hoped that the inception of CAFCASS will bring local managers to the heart of child care policy by conferring membership of the ACPC and other child care groups. This can only assist the practitioner in helping to keep the welfare of the child central. The management of CAFCASS may intervene in cases on behalf of the practitioner to resolve conflict with a local authority. Management intervention may well also assist in preventing delay if effective communications are established between CAFCASS and the local authority, and if issues of good child care practice are central to that relationship.

There is fear that the practitioner, in seeking assistance from a CAFCASS manager, may have their autonomy diluted. As long as there is evidence that the child is central to the thinking of the practitioner advising the court, this should not happen. It is the author's experience that as soon as the child ceases being central, and adult personalities and issues of resources take centre stage, then conflict ensues. An example serves to illustrate this point. As a Panel Manager I received a complaint about the action of a Guardian in writing to a field worker about safety standards and disciplinary practice in a local children's home. The senior manager responsible for all homes became aware of the letter and was furious because it had been sent to a field worker rather than to himself. He admitted that he was angry and the complaint was quickly resolved. It was clear that the guardian had every right to discuss matters that affected a child with the field social worker; the complaint of the local authority manager had not been 'child centred' but to do with the fact that the Guardians actions had upset power relationships and protocol within the local authority.

A child centred culture within CAFCASS is an essential ingredient if the organization is to be successful and effective. It is important here to acknowledge that an imbalance of power could exist if two influential organisations engage in dialogue with each other at the expense of the less powerful individual, the parent. This must be resisted. It is imperative that parents are represented adequately so there will be no danger of them feeling excluded or disadvantaged. To ensure an even playing field parents should bave access to good legal representation. CAFCASS should assist parents by giving them information about solicitors registered on the Law Society's Children Panel.

I shall now return to those situations in which I have had experience of guardians stepping outside the accepted boundaries of their role, and I provide the following case examples.

Non-discriminatory Practice and Valuing Diversity

CAFCASS wishes to promote an organisation which values diversity. The following case study shows how a guardian highlighted discriminatory practice and in consequence had to exceed her role.

Case Study 1

This is an example of a case in which a Guardian had to assess a parent to gain evidence to test her own view that he was capable of parenting his child. The local authority had refused to consider him . . .

The child was a two year old boy who had been accommodated since he was eleven months old. The local authority had applied for a care order with the view to placing the child for adoption. There was a question over the child's paternity and two men were potential fathers. DNA testing was ordered by the court as both men were putting themselves forward as potential carers for the baby, and both considered themselves to be his father. The testing established the biological father and the other man withdrew from the proceedings.

The local authority refused to consider the father as a potential carer. It would not be moved from this position as it believed that he was violent and abused alcohol. This information was provided by the child's mother and was not supported from any other source. The local authority expressed the view that, at 34 years of age, this man had no savings and was still living with his mother. It made the assumption, without evidence, that the paternal grandmother would be the primary carer. At 67 years old the local authority felt that she was too old, even though there had been no assessment of either her state of health, or the extent to which she was proposing to care for her grandchild.

In the light of Standard 7, which requires Guardians to *'positively respond to issues associated with gender, race, culture, religion, language and disability'* (National Standards, 1995), the Guardian felt that the father, and his mother, were being discriminated against on grounds of gender and age. She took the decision to make her own assessment of the couple as she felt that the local authority was not fulfilling its duty to the child by refusing to assess his relatives as potential carers. She clarified that the father did not abuse alcohol, or have a history of violence. She also clarified that the grandmother was not putting herself forward as a primary carer, and would only assist her son in caring for the child. The court accepted the Guardian's assessment and the evidence she gave to undermine the local authority's case. A Residence Order was granted to the father, giving the child the opportunity to remain with his family of birth.

The role of the Guardian is to be aware of discriminatory practice and the case study above is not unusual. However, to date, Panel Managers have not had the opportunity to look at the bigger picture and understand the level of discriminatory practice in a local area. It is an alarming thought that in a local authority this practice could be common place, and the incidents overlooked because of the previous management structure for Guardian Panels. By having an overview of cases the management of CAFCASS will be able to influence the practice of local authorities. By collating examples of discriminatory practice they will be able to bring the matter to the attention of management colleagues running the child and family services of the local authority. This could be through membership of the Area Child Protection Committee and the Family Court Business Committee. Feedback such as this will have enormous benefits locally for children and families, and hopefully will effect change.

Making Decisions without Delay

It is essential to avoid delay in making decisions for children involved in court proceedings and it has been a priority for Guardians to bring this to the court's attention. The authors of the Children Act 1989 recommended that public law proceedings should be completed within three months of the application being lodged. The reality is that most cases are taking up to nine months, or more, and that period is lengthening. Often delay is caused by complexity resulting in the case being transferred to a higher court. The complexity can occur as a result of extended family members wanting to become parties, assessments being completed of potential carers and the number of witnesses that are expected to give evidence at the Final Hearing. The courts are very concerned about delay and are proactive in following the recommendations made in the Booth Report (1996) on delay in public law proceedings before the court. Standard 8, requires that:

> *The Guardian's investigation is undertaken in a competent manner; having been appointed to a particular case, the guardian constructs an initial plan setting out the intended work programme and proceeds to implement it with minimum delay, updating as necessary.*

The *National Standards* (1995) generally outline the role of the Guardian with regard to delay and make it clear that the investigation should be planned, focused and flexible. Matters should be brought back to court at the earliest opportunity if delay is identified.

To date Guardians have had little effective support from Panel Managers on issues of delay and have had to use their own discretion and experience to decide whether to bring matters back to court. CAFCASS will be able to support a practitioner with this decision, through the interdependence of peer and management review. This does however imply that the manager is aware of the complexities of the role of the Guardian. Guardian Panels have been managed by those from different backgrounds; some have been social workers, some lawyers and some administrators. It is important that, where decisions are made by managers in CAFCASS, that they have expertise in child care, whether through working in child care agencies or court welfare. It is equally important that team managers undertake convergence training and use the peer mentoring model to understand the role of a practitioner, in both private and public law, if they are to create a supportive environment for all practitioners.

Case Study 2

This is an example of when a Guardian exceeded their role to bring about a speedy resolution for the children involved, and in doing so prevented delay.

Child A and B were aged five and three respectively. They were children of a mixed heritage. Their mother was white British and their father Chinese Malay. He lived in Penang, Malaysia. The local authority removed the children from the care of their mother under an Emergency Protection Order and applied for a Care Order. The mother was abusing alcohol and placing the children at risk of significant harm.

The father of the children returned to the UK when he heard that the children were in foster care and wanted them to return with him to Penang. His Chinese girl friend and large extended family would be the primary carers while he continued to run his business.

At the time the local authority was at some disadvantage because the case was being kept on duty because of lack of staff. The duty social worker contacted International Social Services (ISS) to ask them to do an assessment of the family, father's girl friend and the services available to the children in Penang. ISS responded that the assessment would take about a year to complete, and they could not guarantee that the person nominated would be a child care professional. It was not in the interests of the children to remain in foster care, and the father had difficulty in remaining in the UK for a year. Rehabilitation to the mother had been ruled out.

The Guardian returned the matter to court and it was agreed that the Guardian herself would complete an assessment in Penang regardless of the local authority's position. After receiving consultation on cultural issues the Guardian spent a week in Penang and completed the assessment with the support of the British Consular Service. Based on the Guardian's evidence, and on expert opinion from a Consultant Psychiatrist, a Residence Order was made to the father and the children were placed outside the jurisdiction of the court.

This case is unusual, but the delay in making decisions for the children would have been unacceptable. Increasingly the staffing crisis in local authority social work has forced Guardians to exceed their role. They possess the skills that are required in the assessment of families and children, and often the Guardian is the most experienced and qualified person dealing with the case. In Case Study 2 the local authority could not provide an assessment within the timetable set by the court. The Guardian was making an independent assessment and could not test out the assessment of the local authority. The local authority accepted the Guardian's assessment and this did cause concern to the mother of the children, who felt that the local authority should have made their own assessment. The boundaries of responsibility became blurred but the alternative of delay for the children would have been harmful.

The Limitations of the Guardian's Role

The final case study in this chapter concerns disposal of a case. It provides an example of when the Guardian would have wanted to exceed the role but the court rules, and legislation, prevented this.

Case Study 3

Child C was made the subject of Care Proceedings in 1996, being then six years old. The threshold criteria were met and a care order was made. Child C had suffered significant emotional harm whilst in the care of her mother. Her mother showed high criticism and low warmth to the little girl and Child C took on the role of carer for her mother, who suffered from mental health vulnerabilities and epilepsy. The mother of the child refused to have her parenting capabilities assessed by the local authority who in response to this applied to the court for a care order.

However during the court proceedings Child C's mother had shown some improvement in her parenting capabilities. A London teaching hospital medical team wanted to continue with a parenting treatment programme. The care plan stated that if the treatment was not successful, or if the mother refused treatment, the child would be removed and a permanent placement sought.

Child C was placed in a respite care placement in June 1999. It was decided not to return the child to her mother. The mother applied to the court in December 1999 for a discharge of the care order. During the investigations the guardian found that the care plan was not followed, and the treatment plan had broken down some weeks after the care order was made. Child C remained with her mother even though other agencies were bringing to the attention of social services Child C's distress and unhappiness. For one year Child C did not have an allocated social worker and, as a result, the child's circumstances deteriorated.

The Guardian was very critical of the local authority and felt that the child had been failed by the care system and by the agencies involved with her care. The proceedings ended in July 2000 and Child C was then ten years old. The consultant psychiatrist who had been responsible for the child's care in 1996 was of the opinion that Child C would probably not recover from the emotional harm meted out to her by her mother. The family placement team in turn felt that Child C would be a difficult child to place and they could not give a time scale for placement.

The case was heard in the High Court and the Judge was also very concerned about the conduct of the local authority. The mother withdrew her application as she agreed under cross examination that she was unable to care for Child C because of ill health. There was no legal way the Guardian could remain in the case to ensure that resources were spent to expedite a permanent placement for Child C. The Guardian felt that Child C had grounds to make a claim against the local authority for negligence. The Judge ordered the Guardian to write to the Official Solicitor about her concerns. He ordered the release of the relevant court reports concerned with both the care proceedings and the discharge of care proceedings so that the Official Solicitor could consider the issue of negligence.

The Guardian although aware that the court had recognised her concerns, felt frustrated that she left the case without a satisfactory outcome for the child. Not only had the Guardian's duties finished under the existing court rules but so had those of the child's solicitor. Under the support aspect of CAFCASS it may be possible to counter this frustration for the practitioner.

A Role for CAFCASS

CAFCASS will be able to have an overview of cases and perhaps even research the outcomes for children such as Child C. It became evident to the Guardian in Case Study 3 that there was little expertise available in taking matters further when negligence is identified. In my role as Panel Manager I have been sometimes told in retrospect about cases where the Guardian has felt that the child protection process has failed the child but where the Guardian felt unable to take the matter further, because of the lack of knowledge of how to deal with cases such as these. CAFCASS has promised that through Information Technology the sharing of information will be a priority[110] and therefore children before the courts will enjoy a high quality service that is consistent throughout the country. Those that manage the service need to have an overview of those cases that cause practitioners concern, in order that they can advise on the action that should be taken on behalf of the child. A national overview of such cases would also inform practice within local authorities.

Guardians do not exceed their role lightly and often in the past they made a decision in isolation. They have been left to explain it in retrospect to a manager either as a result of a complaint, or during an appraisal or re-appointment interview. This retrospective management of cases has been difficult for both the practitioner and manager. The practitioner has been put in a position of having to justify stepping outside the boundaries of the role for something that at the time seemed the best decision, and which created a positive outcome for the child. It is so much better to have management support when the decision is taken to exceed the role, or at least to be able to take advice about the merits of such an action.

Over the last eight years of being a Panel Manager I have never been asked by a Guardian for consultancy over the issue of exceeding their role, although many times I have been asked to resource consultancy over other practice issues. The legislative framework of the Guardian service created a culture within which there was no trust that managers would be sympathetic to pushing at the boundaries of Guardian's roles, and it seemed that the Guardians would rather 'face the music' if the matter came to light, than discuss such matters with a Panel Manager. Under CAFCASS, by being more transparent about exceeding their role, individual practitioners should gain better support if the matter is discussed and agreed by the organisation, especially if a complaint should be raised about the matter at a later stage.

If complaints are made against CAFCASS, rather than against individuals, then this too should bring benefits to those working in the organisation. Complaints about the Guardian service have until now not been viewed as an opportunity to review practice on a wider level because they have always been so personal, and because Guardians have felt at a professional and personal disadvantage. Although the Panel Managers tried to adopt a position of neutrality when investigating complaints, Guardians, being individually responsible for their practice, felt isolated. Also before resolution, and sometimes afterwards, Guardians did not want the matter to be discussed with other members of the panel. It is my experience on the

---

[110] David Lye, Project Director CAFCASS Takes Shape. *Seen and Heard* Volume 10 Issue 3 (2000).

Hertfordshire Panel that most complaints were resolved at an early stage. The person that does offer the Guardian support is often the solicitor for the child. In writing a supportive letter on behalf of the Guardian, they can on some occasions, provide information that helps to resolve the matter. On other occasions however, such letters have brought a litigious feel that is not always helpful. However, it must be said that Guardians, because of their individual accountability, have been vulnerable, and this has made them targets for criticism from the other parties in the proceedings.

There have been examples when parties want to try and review the decisions of the court through the complaints procedure, or to try to change a Guardian's recommendation. Panel Managers have always stressed the point that the Guardians' professional judgement is their own, but sometimes complainants are determined to ensure that the matter is investigated as fully as possible.

Panel Managers have also had to withstand pressure from the local authority, their own employers and often senior officers, to intervene in cases to help change the mind of the Guardian. On one occasion I had the experience of refusing the request of a misguided manager, that I have a quiet word with the judge about overturning the Guardian's recommendation, in order to side step a complaint!

Although complaints must be welcomed by organisations, and of course, *some* have been upheld, nevertheless Guardians have lost income while they endeavour to answer a complaint from a vexatious complainant. It has become a yearly event for one Panel or another to change their complaints procedure trying to achieve a balance of fairness for the complainant and the practitioner. It is to be hoped that in CAFCASS, complaints will be seen more as an opportunity for the service to develop than as a threat to the individual practitioner.

Conclusion

If these three case studies are recognised as common place by Guardians, it must be argued that such cases needed to be correlated. The bigger picture of discriminatory practice, delay and failure to protect children must be presented to an audience that can bring about change in the interests of children. The indications are that those that lead CAFCASS want to foster a team approach to the work.

The management and practitioners of CAFCASS need to work together to develop a service for children and families. To be able to work in this way there must be a shift in culture from one of independence to interdependence. Teams that perform to a high standard of practice are not built over night, and trust and respect for each other's skills and knowledge has to develop. It is true to say that Guardian Panels have not worked as high performing teams, but as high performing individuals. It is going to be a challenge to change the culture of these high performing individuals to become committed members of high performing teams.

Teams have to work together to take on the responsibility of the whole and not the parts. Those high performing individuals may have to take responsibility not only for the success, but the failure, of a team that has not reached targets set by CAFCASS. The team approach can only work if the targets set are not dictated by management, but agreed by the practitioners. All within the team need to see themselves as equal partners, wherever they sit in the organisation, and a valuable example of this is the southern region appraisers group who have worked side by side with management.

Success then can breed success within the organisation. Teams such as these can only be effective if a commitment to specific goals, a common approach and a meaningful purpose are all in place. Finally, each member of the team needs to be accountable to the others *and* to the organisation. The rewards are that for the organisation the work will be done to a high standard, for the team there will be a feeling of high morale and for the individual, personal growth. The high performance ethic has been part of the culture of the former Guardian service, and it is this strength that it brings to CAFCASS. The challenge now is to transfer this ethic to the multi-skilled teams. The overall reward must be that a clearer picture of child care practice in the UK emerges, and that CAFCASS can influence this on a national scale.

10 Human Rights and Family Law

Penelope Wood

Introduction

This chapter explores the background to the enactment of the Human Rights Act 1998 and looks at some of the case law of the European Court of Human Rights which illustrates the interpretation and implementation of Convention Rights. It also discusses the likely impact on Public Law Proceedings of the Human Rights Act which came into force on 2 October 2000.

Historic Background

On 5 May 1949 the Council of Europe was created to promote European Unity. The European Convention on Human Rights and Fundamental Freedoms is an international treaty which seeks to protect individuals from arbitrary interference by the State. It applies to those European states that are members of the Council of Europe. There are currently 41 member states including the UK who have ratified the Convention. The Council established the European Commission of Human Rights to consider complaints from individuals that their Convention rights had been breached. If found admissable the complainant and their Government would be invited to reach a friendly settlement. If the parties were unable to reach a settlement the Commission might refer the matter to the European Court of Human Rights for hearing and judgment. As of 1 November 1998 the Commission and the Court were replaced with a single European Court of Human Rights which now sits full time in Strasbourg.

Vertical Duties and Horizontal Rights

In addition to protecting individuals from state interference ('vertical duties') the European Court has held in relation to Article 8 (respect for family life) that the State must also protect one private individual against interference in his Convention rights by another individual ('horizontal rights'). Thus when considering family law applications the courts must consider the competing Convention rights of all parties[111].

Some Convention rights are unqualified; e.g. Article 3: prohibition of torture, Article 4: prohibition of slavery and forced labour. Others, including Articles 8–11, set out the right and then are followed by a second part

---

[111] *Marckz* v. *Belgium* 2 EHRR 330 para 31, and *X and Y* v. *The Netherlands* 8 EHRR 235 p360.

describing how the right may need to be limited. The European Court of Human Rights has made clear that in relation to some Convention rights, particularly those requiring a balance between competing considerations, a measure of discretion will be allowed to the domestic authorities. This is referred to as 'the margin of appreciation'.

Principles Justifying Interference by the State

There are four underlying principles which have become settled in Convention case law as justifying an interference with a Convention right. These are that the interference must be:

1. in accordance with the law
2. serve a legitimate aim
3. be necessary in a democratic society
4. not be discriminatory

The case of *Scott* v. *UK*, illustrates these principles. This was an application by a UK mother who contended that her right to family life under Article 8 had been breached. The applicant mother was alcoholic. She gave birth to a girl in 1991 and her daughter's name was placed on the 'at risk' register. The mother continued drinking to excess. Care proceedings were initiated. Twelve interim care orders were made whilst the local authority attempted rehabilitation. In 1993 the mother had a serious relapse and in June of that year the court made a final care order with a care plan for rehabilitation. However, in September 1993, the local authority held a meeting (the mother was not invited to attend) and a decision was made to abandon the attempt to rehabilitate the girl with her mother. In October 1994 the County Court granted the local authority's application to dispense with the mother's consent to free the child for adoption.

The mother complained to the European Court of Human Rights that the local authority had failed to look at her case properly in September 1993 and the lack of consultation thereafter resulted in the decision in October 1994 to dispense with her agreement to free the child for adoption. Both the mother and the Government accepted that the authorities and the County Court had acted in accordance with domestic law and that the interference with the applicant's right under Article 8 pursued at least one legitimate aim, the protection of the rights of the child. What was contested by the parties was whether the interference was 'necessary' in a democratic society.

The European Court held that it must consider the case as a whole. As regards the merits, the Court considered that it could not be questioned that the mother could not care for the child as she had not rid herself of her alcohol problem. The domestic court had considered that it would be detrimental to the child to continue in a temporary placement. The domestic court could not be criticised for concluding that the child should be freed for adoption and the interference was necessary in a democratic society.

Undoubtedly consideration of what is in the best interests of the child is always of crucial importance. In these circumstances, it must also be born in mind that the national authorities have the benefit of direct contact with all the persons concerned, often at the very stage when care measures are being envisaged or immediately after their implementation. It follows from these considerations that the Court's task is not to take the place of the competent national authorities in the exercise of their responsibilities for the regulation of the public care of children and the rights of parents whose children are taken into care, but rather to review under the Convention the decisions taken by those authorities in the exercise of their power of appreciation. The margin of appreciation to be accorded to the competent national authorities will vary in the light of the nature of the issues and the seriousness of the interests at stake. Thus the Court recognises that the authorities enjoy a wide margin of appreciation in assessing the necessity of taking a child into care. However, stricter scrutiny is required for any further limitations, such as restrictions placed by those authorities on parental rights and access, or on the legal safeguards designed to secure the effective protection of the right of parents and children to respect for their family life, where such further limitations might entail the danger that the family relations between the parents and a young child are effectively curtailed[112].

Protection of health and morals

In public law proceedings the State's motivation for interfering with the parent's and child's right to family life will be for the protection of 'health or morals' of the child. Where the Court is satisfied on hearing evidence that the threshold criteria imposed by s 31 (a) Children Act 1989 are met, such interference is likely to be seen as justified. The State must also demonstrate that the interference is fair and proportionate to the need to protect. Taking a child into care is to be regarded as a temporary measure. The obligation is upon the authorities to rehabilitate a child with its parents if it is achievable within a realistic timetable to meet the needs of the child[113]. The obligation to endeavour to rehabilitate is not absolute. There is a need to balance the rights of all those concerned in the decision, particularly those of the child. Where a child is in long term care, severe and lasting restrictions on access may be found to not be proportionate to the legitimate aims pursued.

Breach of Convention Rights and amending legislation

In order to make application to the European Commission and ultimately to the European Court of Human Rights the applicant had to claim to be 'a victim of a violation'. In general, complaints should not have been

---

[112] *Scott* v. *UK* [2000] 1 FLR at 968 para G.
[113] *Eriksson* v. *Sweden* 12 EHRR 259 paras 81 and 83.

submitted before all effective domestic remedies had been exhausted. Where the European Court finds a violation of the Convention has occurred it is required to consider whether the applicant is entitled to any compensation and costs. The Court cannot order anything other than compensation and costs. In many instances the Court decides that finding a violation has occurred is in itself 'just satisfaction' for the applicant. It cannot order the state to take or refrain from taking any particular action. However the finding that domestic law is in breach of an Article of the Convention may lead the Government to redress the breach by amendment of the law or the passing of new legislation.

In *Gaskin* v. *UK*[114] the applicant was in the care of Liverpool social services from 1959–1977. He alleged he had been abused whilst in care. To overcome his problems and deal with his past he asked to see his files. The local authority successfully argued against disclosure claiming public interest immunity. The Judge of first instance found in favour of the local authority by balancing the public interest in the proper operation of the child care service with the needs of the individual and public interest in reviewing the standard of care of the local authority: if writers of reports knew they were likely to be disclosed they might be reluctant to be frank. The Court of Appeal supported the Judge's ruling and ordered disclosure of only 65 out of 352 documents. The applicant made complaint that the refusal of full disclosure amounted to a breach of Article 8. The European Court of Human Rights found that, as the file compiled and maintained by the local authority related to the basic identity of the applicant's formative years, refusal to allow access was an interference with his right to respect for private life. There was however a wide margin of appreciation or levels of differentiation (see below) to be applied in the balance between the competing interest of the child care system and the applicant's record of his personal history. The confidentiality of the contents of the file contributed to the effective operation of the child care system and was a legitimate aim. As a consequence of this ruling the domestic law was subsequently changed and the Access to Personal Files (Social Services) Regulations 1989 were made which impose a duty to disclose such documents to the individuals concerned, subject to some limitations which includes inter alia information prohibited by the Adoption Act 1976 and information which may be the subject of legal privilege (Regulation 9).

The Human Rights Act 1998 (HRA)

This Act was passed incorporating Convention Rights into UK domestic law. It provides that domestic law be enacted, interpreted and amended so that it is compatible with the Convention. As a result, from 2 October 2000 an individual can enforce the Convention rights against the state in the domestic courts. Section 8 of the Act provides that a court or tribunal, where

---

[114] *The Gaskin Case* [1990] 1 FLR 167.

it finds an authority has acted unlawfully, may grant such relief or remedy or make such order within its powers as it considers appropriate. A damages award is likely to only be available through the civil courts as it is doubtful whether family courts have such jurisdiction. The Human Rights Act 1998 has not incorporated all the Articles of the Convention, for example neither Article 1 (obligation to respect human rights), nor Article 13 (right to an effective domestic remedy) have been included.

Retrospective application

Section 22 (4) HRA 1998 provides that where proceedings are brought by or at the instigation of a public authority, a person who claims he is a victim of an unlawful act committed by a public authority under Section 6 (1)[115] may rely on Convention rights in any legal proceedings whenever that alleged unlawful act took place, but otherwise the Human Rights Act does not apply to an act which took place prior to Section 7 (1) (b)[116] which came into force on 2 October 2000.

The Human Rights Act applies in public law proceedings to the functions of courts, tribunals, local authorities and social services departments. It also applies to private bodies with a public role, for example the NSPCC who are authorised under section 31(a) of the Children Act to apply for a Care Order. It is also likely to apply to the Official Solicitor and to Guardians ad litem appointed to represent children in a care case as they are representing a child through their statutory role. Public authorities must act compatibly with the Convention rights unless statutory provisions prevent it. Subordinate legislation which is found to be incompatible with Convention rights can be disapplied or quashed unless it is 'inevitably incompatible' (s3 and s4).

Higher Courts may make a declaration that primary legislation is incompatible with Convention rights, but the legislation will stand until repealed or amended. A Minister can amend the offending legislation by Order (s10).

Article 3 of the Convention

Local authorities are charged with the protection of children under the Parts IV and V of the Children Act 1989. The state has a positive obligation to protect children from inhuman and degrading treatment under Article 3 of the Convention. Thus a local authority will be justified in taking care

---

[115]Section 6 (1) 'It is unlawful for a public authority to act in a way which is incompatible with a Convention Right'.

[116]Section 7 (1) 'A person who claims that a public authority has acted (or proposes to act) in a way which is made unlawful by Section 6 (1) may:
(a) bring proceedings against the authority under this Act in the appropriate Court or Tribunal;
(b) rely on the Convention right or rights concerned in any legal proceedings, but only if he is (or would be) a victim of an unlawful act.

proceedings to remove a child from its family to prevent such treatment. Care proceedings where the threshold criteria of section 31 Children Act 1989 are met are likely to be 'necessary' for the protection of the health or morals of the child.

Articles 6 and 8 of the Convention

Of the Articles of the Convention which are incorporated into domestic law, those which will have the greatest impact in family proceedings are Article 6 and Article 8:

> Article 6:
> 1. In the determination of his civil rights and obligations or of any criminal charge against him, everyone is entitled to a fair and public hearing within a reasonable time by an independent and impartial tribunal established by the law. Judgement shall be pronounced publicly but the press and public may be excluded from all or part of the trial in the interests of morals. public order or national security in a democratic society, where the interests of juveniles or the protection of the private life of the parties so require, or to the extent strictly necessary in the opinion of the court in special circumstances where publicity would prejudice the interests of justice.

The allegation against a parent that the threshold criteria of section 31(a) Children Act 1989 is met in care proceedings is comparable to a charge of criminal offence and thus a parent will have the specific rights set out in parts 2 and 3 of Article 6.

> 2. Everyone charged with a criminal offence shall be presumed innocent until proved guilty according to the law.
> 3. Everyone charged with a criminal offence has the following minimum rights:
>   a. To be informed promptly, in a language which he understands and in detail of the nature and cause of the accusation against him.
>   b. To have adequate time and facilities for the preparation of his defence.
>   c. To defend himself in person or through legal assistance of his own choosing or, if he has not sufficient means to pay for legal assistance, to be given it free when the interests of justice so require.
>   d. To examine or have examined witnesses against him and to obtain the attendance and examination of witnesses on his behalf under the same conditions as witnesses against him.
>   e. To have the free assistance of an interpreter if he cannot understand or speak the language of the court.

Article 8
1. Everyone has the right to respect for his private and family life,
   his home and his correspondence.
2. There shall be no interference by a public authority with the
   exercise of this right except such as is in accordance with the law
   and is necessary in a democratic society in the interest of national
   security, public safety or the economic well-being of the country,
   for the prevention of disorder or crime, for the protection of
   health or morals, or for the protection of the rights and freedoms
   of others.

The Concept of Family Life

When considering the application of Article 8 it will be necessary to consider
what is meant by the concept of 'family life' and who benefits from it. The
answer to the question is continually evolving. Married parents always have
a right to family life and this will not cease on separation or divorce.

Unmarried Fathers

In the case of *Keegan* v. *Ireland*[117], an unmarried Irish father made
application to the Court alleging breach of Article 8. He had cohabited with
his girlfriend for a year when she became pregnant. The couple had planned
to marry but the relationship broke down. Their child was born after they
had separated. The child was placed for adoption without his knowledge.
The relevant provisions of the Adoption Act 1952 allowed the adoption of
the child without the father's consent. The father applied to the Court under
the Guardianship of Infants Act 1964 to be appointed the child's guardian
which would enable him to challenge the adoption. He was appointed
guardian and awarded custody of the child.

The High Court upheld the decision of the lower Court but the Supreme
Court ruled that the wishes of the natural father should not be considered
if the prospective adopters could make significantly better provisions for the
child's welfare. The case was remitted to the High Court. By this time the
child had been with the prospective adopters for a year. The High Court
found that if removed from the adopters the child would be likely to suffer
trauma and have difficulties in forming relationships of trust. The High
Court therefore refused to appoint the father guardian and the adoption
order was made.

The father made complaint to the Commission on two grounds, a) that
there had been a breach of Article 8 and b) that there had been a breach of
Article 6 in that the father had been deprived of *locus standi* in the adoption
proceedings.

The Commission found that there had been a breach of Article 8: the
notion of family was not solely confined to marriage. A child born to parents

---

[117] *Keegan* v. *Ireland* [1994] Series A No 290.

who had a relationship which included cohabitation is part of the 'family unit' for the purposes of Article 8 even where, by the time of the birth, the parents are no longer cohabiting. The fact that Irish law permitted the secret placement of a child for adoption without the applicant's knowledge or consent and the subsequent making of the adoption order amounted to a breach of the applicant's right to family life.

In *McMichael* v. *UK*[118] the male applicant complained that as a result of his status as an unmarried father in Scottish law he had no parental rights from the moment of the child's birth and no right to participate in the freeing proceedings which followed the child being placed in care. The Court rejected his complaint under Article 14[119] and Article 8:

> *According to the Court's well established case-law, a difference of treatment is discriminatory if it has no reasonable and objective justification, that is, if it does not pursue a legitimate aim or if there is not a reasonable relationship of proportionality between the means employed and the aim sought to be realised.*

As the Commission remarked:

> *It is axiomatic that the nature of the relationships of natural fathers with the children will inevitably vary from ignorance and indifference at one end of the spectrum to a close and stable relationship indistinguishable from the conventional matrimonial-based family unit at the other.*

More recently the difference in status recognised by the Children Act was confirmed as being Convention compliant. In the case of *B* v. *UK*[120], an unmarried father applied for a parental responsibility order and a contact order. The mother removed the child from England to Italy. The English courts dismissed the father's application under the Hague Convention on the Civil Aspects of International Child Abduction 1980 on the basis that he did not have any formal custody rights under English Law. The father made complaint to the European Court that unmarried fathers were discriminated against in the protection given to their relationships with their children by comparison with the protection given to married fathers. The Court declared the complaint inadmissable. It was held that there is objective and reasonable justification for the differences in treatment between married and unmarried fathers.

Grandparents, relatives and siblings

Grandparents and other relatives may have a right to family life depending on the circumstances. Each case will be examined on its merits to determine

---

[118]20 EHRR 205.
[119]Article 14 Prohibition of discrimination.
[120]*B* v. *UK* [2000] 1 FLR 1.

whether there are sufficient links[121]. The rights of children under Article 8 extend to their relationship with their siblings. This will of course be relevant in situations where siblings may be split as a result of care proceedings: one sibling returning to the care of their parent or parents and another being placed for fostering or adoption, or placed separately.

In the case of *Boyle* v. *UK*[122], application was made by the uncle of a boy who was removed into care following accusations of sexual abuse against his mother who was arrested but not prosecuted. Although the care court found that he had been a good father figure to the boy, the uncle's repeated requests for access were refused as he continued to deny the sexual abuse by his sister. He was not invited to attend any case conferences.

The uncle contended that prior to the coming into force of the Children Act 1989 there was no right of access for non-parental relatives which was a breach of Article 8. In a majority decision (14–4) the European Court found:

1. Cohabitation was not a pre-requisite for the maintenance of family life.
2. Where parents are denied access to a child, in general there is an interference with family life: this was not necessarily so with other close relatives as their access is normally at the discretion of the parents or guardians. Here where all contact was terminated there was an interference.
3. The interference was in accordance with the law for the purpose of safeguarding the child's health and rights within the meaning of Article 8 (2).
4. Although an uncle would not require as much involvement in the decision making process as a parent, there was no attempt to reach a compromise and allow meaningful dialogue with the uncle. The interference was therefore *not* necessary *in the sense of proportion* and there was a breach of Article 8.

In domestic law, where a care order is made the parental discretion as to which close relatives a child should have contact with passes to the local authority. A grandparent has no right to be heard within care proceedings, or once a care order has been made, to apply for a contact order under section 34 without leave of the Court, unless the grandparent falls within the categories set out in section 34 (b) (c) or (d). Likewise a grandparent has no right to become party to adoption proceedings. It is possible that this may lead to challenge as a breach of Article 8 where a grandparent can demonstrate a sufficient link to the child, perhaps by being part of the same household.

In considering whether there is a breach of Article 8 it is necessary to ask:

1. *Is there an interference in family life?* Inevitably the answer will be yes, where public law applications are made under the Children Act 1989.

---

[121] *Marckx* v. *Belgium* above para 40.
[122] *Boyle* v. *UK* [1994] 19 EHRR 179.

2. *Is the interference in accordance with the law?* Providing court procedures
are followed it is highly unlikely that the interference will be found not
to be in accordance with the law, unless there has a been a declaration
that the statute in question is incompatible with the Convention.
3. *Does the interference pursue a legitimate aim?* In public law cases the local
authority will inevitably have a legitimate aim: to protect the child.
4. *Is the interference necessary in a democratic society?* The welfare of the
child becomes relevant when the Court is considering whether the
interference with the parent's rights is justified as necessary.

The Margin of Appreciation

A wide margin of appreciation is allowed by the European Court of Human
Rights when considering whether there has been a breach of Article 8. The
Court will consider the complaint in the context of traditions about the role
of family life in the country of the complainant. Clearly there will be
considerable differences in *mores*, the role of local authority intervention,
and resources, between one country and another.

The most likely ground for challenging the making of a care order is that
it has not been shown to be 'necessary'. This may be relevant when a parent
could, with considerable input from the local authority, meet the child's
needs but the local authority does not have resources available.

Where a challenge is to be mounted that the local authority plan for care
is not necessary, relying on Article 8, it should be raised at the Final Hearing
as a reason for the judge not to make a care order. Alternatively, it can be
raised at appeal by arguing that the court at first instance did not act in
accordance with its duty under the Human Rights Act, the duty to interpret
legislation, where possible, in the light of the Human Rights Act.

The Need to Involve Parents in Decision Making

Case law shows that the decision-making process which leads to the
interference in family life must be fair and afford due respect to family life.
This is illustrated by the case of *W* v. *UK*[123] a case which predates the
Children Act 1989.

W's son had been placed in voluntary foster care at the age of 12 months.
The local authority made a Parental Rights Resolution[124] which was agreed
at the time by the parents as it was temporary. The local authority then
decided to place the child in long term foster care with a view to adoption.

---

[123] *W* v. *UK* [1988] 10 EHRR 29.
[124] Prior to the implementation of the Children Act 1989, the local authority were able to assume
parental rights by means of a Parental Rights Resolution in a number of events including
where a child's parents were dead and he had no guardian or custodian, or that his parents
had abandoned him, or suffered from some permanent disability or mental disorder, or were
of such habits or mode of life as to be unfit to have the care of the child, or had so
consistently failed without reasonable cause to discharge the obligations of a parent as to be
unfit to have the care of a child [Child Care Act 1980 section 3].

The parents were informed of this and a further decision was made that their access to the child should be limited and later terminated. The parents personal position improved dramatically. They therefore applied for the rescinding of the resolution by the Juvenile Court. Upon their successful application the local authority immediately warded the child to freeze the child's placement with his foster parents. By the time the delayed proceedings were concluded the child was two years old. As a result the Court decided that the child should remain with the foster carers and access be terminated.

The European Court of Human Rights found a breach of Article 8. The Court held that the mutual enjoyment by parent and child of each other's company was fundamental to the right to family life. When a child is taken into care the natural family relationship remains. Decisions as to restriction of access constitute interference and often have irreversible effect. There is therefore a need for protection from arbitrary interference which allows the court to look at the process itself. The parents must be involved in the decision-making process to a degree sufficient to provide them with the requisite protection of their interest. The views of the parents must be taken into account and they must be allowed to take advantage of any remedies available to them.

In *Scott* v. *UK*[125], the European Court of Human Rights has found that giving family members the right to make representations at case conferences, and the facility to seek review of decisions, is an acceptable level of consultation. A parent must always be consulted prior to a child being placed on the Child Protection Register.

Duty to Facilitate Rehabilitation of Child with Parents

European Case law stresses that Care Orders should be seen as temporary measures. In *Hokkanen* v. *Finland*[126], the Judge said:

> *What is decisive is whether the national authorities have taken all reasonable steps to facilitate reunion as can reasonably be demanded in the special circumstances of the case.*

In this case, the applicant's wife died when their child was two years old. The child was sent to live with the maternal grandparents on a temporary basis. When the time came for the child to be returned, the grandparents refused and legal proceedings were commenced. The court ordered interim contact but the grandparents refused to comply and appealed, which took time. In the interim the child remained with them. Requests were made for coercive measures but these were not acted upon. The proceedings went on until the child was ten years old, by which time the court decided it was better for the

---

[125][2000] 1 FLR 969.
[126][1996] 1 FLR 289.

child to stay with her grandparents and custody was transferred to them. The applicant had only ever been allowed contact on a few occasions.

The applicant complained that the refusal to enforce the court orders and the eventual transfer of the child to the grandparents was a violation of Article 8. The Commission found a breach of Article 8, and held that:

1. The object of Article 8 is to protect the individual from arbitrary interference by public authorities and to support the positive obligations inherent in an effective 'respect' for family life. A balance has to be struck between the interests of the individual and the community as a whole.
2. The obligation to facilitate reunion is not absolute since the reunion may not be able to take place immediately. The right to coercion is limited since the interests and freedoms of all concerned must be considered, particularly the best interests of the child.
3. The later transfer of custody from the father to the grandparents was 'in accordance' with the law, pursued a legitimate aim of protecting the right of the child and was necessary in a democratic society. The domestic Court did not overstep the margin of appreciation and the measure was not disproportionate to the legitimate aim of protecting the child.

   Thus although the European Court found a breach of Article 8 in respect of the non-enforcement of the contact order, they did not find there had been a breach of Article 8 with regard to the non-enforcement of the father's right to custody.

Applications Under Section 38 (6) Children Act 1989

The argument that local authorities are obliged to facilitate rehabilitation can be used when seeking an assessment by application under section 38 (6) Children Act 1989 where the local authority is reluctant to allow, or fund, a residential assessment. The Court will expect the authorities to have carried out extensive assessment prior to embarking on a care plan for permanence with an alternative family.

In *Johansen* v. *Norway*[127] the applicant was another whose child was taken into care when he was 12 years old due to concerns about his health and development. The applicant gave birth to a daughter shortly afterwards and, due to the state of health of the applicant, this child was immediately taken into foster care. The child was placed with a view to adoption, access terminated and the applicant's parental rights removed. Eventually the applicant's 12 year old son came back to live with her. The applicant mother later had two further children who lived with her. All appeals requesting the return of her daughter failed.

The applicant mother complained that there was a violation of her right to respect for family life on account of the Care Order, the termination of access, the deprivation of her parental rights and the length of the proceedings.

---

[127] *Johansen* v. *Norway* 23 EHRR 33.

The Commission declared the application admissable and expressed the opinion that there was a violation of Article 8 in respect of the removal of her parental rights and deprivation of access. However they did not find a violation in respect of the care order nor a breach of Article 6 or Article 13[128]. The Court in upholding the decision of the Commission held that there is a wide margin of appreciation in assessing the necessity of taking a child into care, but a stricter scrutiny is called for with any further limitations such as restrictions placed by those authorities on parental rights and access.

The taking of the applicant's daughter into care and the continuation of the care decision were based on reasons which were not only relevant, but also sufficient for the purposes of Article 8. They were supported by painstaking and detailed assessments by experts. The European Court will not substitute its view for that of the national court as to the relative weight to be given to that evidence. The state acted within the margin of appreciation and there was no violation. However, the deprivation of parental rights and access were far reaching measures, totally depriving the applicant of her family life with the child and inconsistent with the aim of reuniting them. Such measure should only be applied in exceptional circumstances motivated by an overriding requirement pertaining to the child's best interests.

Duty of Local Authority to Promote Contact

The local authority has a positive duty to promote contact between the child and their parents and anyone else who has a right to family life in respect of that child. This duty is echoed in the provisions of section 34 of the Children Act 1989: subsection 1 being in mandatory terms:

> *where a child is in the care of the local authority, the local authority shall (subject to the provisions of section 34) allow the child reasonable contact with his parents, any guardian or any person who immediately before the care order had a residence order.*

The starting point in the balancing exercise is that the rights of the child have no special status, although the child too has a right to respect for his family and private life under Article 8. The parents have rights under Article 8 which *prima facie* entitle them to continue contact with the child in care. If there are no overriding reasons for restricting, or even in the exceptional case, for terminating, parental contact for reasons of the welfare of the child the Court would in principle countenance such interference if, following judicial scrutiny the reasons for it were 'relevant and sufficient'[129].

In *Olsson* v. *Sweden*[130] a violation of Article 8 was found only in the manner in which the decision regarding contact was implemented. The

---

[128] Article 6: Right to a fair trial; Article 13: Right to an effective remedy.
[129] Johansen case 23 EHRR 29.
[130] *Olsson* v. *Sweden* 11 EHRR 259.

applicants were the parents of three children. The parents had parenting difficulties. The children were taken into care on a provisional basis. At a later hearing where medical and psychological reports were available they were taken into care permanently. The parents were found to be incapable of caring for them. Various appeals followed. Due to administrative difficulties the three children were placed separately in foster homes at a considerable distance from each other and their parents. Contact was limited. Appeals against the contact decisions were made right through the courts, the applicants being legally represented throughout. The applicants complained that the decision to take the children into care, the manner in which it had been implemented and the refusal to allow contact gave rise to violations of Article 8.

The Court found that there was a breach of Article 8 in the manner of the decision to place the children in care but not in the decision itself. 'Splitting up a family is a very serious interference which must be supported by sufficiently sound and weighty considerations in the interests of the child. It is not sufficient that the child would be better off if placed in care.' As there were no adoption applications, the care decision was temporary with the ultimate aim of reuniting the family. The distance of the placements and the separation of the children was an impediment to that aim, compounded by the restriction on parental access.

Secure Accommodation

Under Article 5 everyone has a right to liberty and security of person. The right is not absolute. Paragraph 4 of Article 5 states that:

> . . . *everyone who is deprived of his liberty by arrest or detention shall be entitled to take proceedings by which the lawfulness of his detention shall be decided speedily by a court and his release ordered if the detention is not lawful.*

The recent decision in *Re AS (Secure Accommodation Order)* [1999] 1 FLR 103 is of interest in this respect. Mrs Justice Bracewell allowed an appeal against the making of a secure accommodation order by a Stipendiary Magistrate. The child was not present at the hearing although represented by solicitor and counsel. The child had not had notice of the proceedings and no Guardian ad litem had been appointed. The making of a secure accommodation order involved the deprivation of liberty and it was implicit that the child's position should be properly represented in court. Legal representation must involve the taking of instructions. Mrs Justice Bracewell distinguished the case of *Re W* [1994] 2 FLR 1092. In *Re W* Mr Justice Ewbank exercised his discretion to refuse to allow the child concerned to attend court, but dealt explicitly with the need for counsel and solicitors to be able to take instructions from the child so as to be able to present the child's case before the Court. Mrs Justice Bracewell considered this sufficient to comply with Article 6.

Consent to Medical Treatment

A child who has attained the age of 16 years is capable of giving consent to his own treatment, whether it be surgical, medical or dental[131]. The decision in the *Gillick* case[132] makes clear that even prior to the age of 16 years a child will have the right to consent or refuse to consent to treatment if he has sufficient understanding and intelligence and is capable of making up his own mind on the matter requiring decision. The Children Act Guidance, Vol 3, Family Placements, para 2.32 states that the responsible authority should draw the child's attention to their rights to give or refuse consent to examination or treatment if they are 16 or over, or if they are under 16 and the doctor considers the child sufficiently able to understand the consequences of consent or refusal. However a parent or local authority holding parental responsibility may under domestic law over-rule a *Gillick* competent child's refusal of medical treatment. In such circumstances there may be a breach of the child's rights under Article 8 or, depending on the reasons for refusal of medical treatment, of Article 9[133].

The court can give consent for a child's medical treatment. The test applied by the court is as to whether the giving of consent, following a parent's refusal to do so, is in the best interests of the child. Inevitably in grappling with such problems the court may need to consider the competing human rights of several individuals. The poignant case of the conjoined twins in September 2000[134], brought the dilemma of such a balancing exercise into sharp focus. The parents had refused permission for the doctors to attempt separation of the twins which would result in one twin's inevitable death, although the other twin was thought to have expectations of a reasonable quality of life. If the twins were not separated it was likely both would die within a short time as the weaker twin was relying on the stronger twin's heart and lungs for oxygen.

Lord Robert Walker summarised:

'(iii) Mary has a right to life[135], under the common law of England (based as it is on Judeo-Christian foundations) and under the

---

[131] FLRA 1969 s 8(1).
[132] *Gillick* v. *West Norfolk and Wisbech Health Authority and Another* [1986] 1 AC 112.
[133] Article 9: Freedom of thought, conscience and religion.
[134] Draft judgment of Court Appeal in *Re A (children)* available via internet at htp:/ wood.ceta.gov/uk/courtser/judgments.nsf/863c6413.
[135] Article 2: 1. Everyone's life shall be protected by law. No one shall be deprived of his life intentionally save in the execution of a sentence of a court following his conviction of a crime for which this penalty is provided by law.
2. Deprivation of life shall not be regarded as inflicted in contravention of this Article when it results from the use of force which is no more than absolutely necessary:
(a) in defence of any person from unlawful violence;
(b) in order to effect a lawful arrest or to prevent the escape of a person lawfully detained;
(c) in action lawfully taken for the purpose of quelling a riot or insurrection.

European Convention on Human Rights. It would be unlawful to kill Mary intentionally, that is to undertake an operation with the primary purpose of killing her.

(iv) But Jodie also has a right to life.

(v)   Every human being's right to life carries with it, as an intrinsic part of it, rights of bodily integrity and autonomy: the right to have one's own body whole and intact and (on reaching an age of understanding) to take decisions about one's own body.

(vi) By a rare and tragic mischance, Mary and Jodie have both been deprived of the bodily integrity and autonomy which is their natural right. There is a strong presumption that an operation to separate them would be in the best interests of each of them. In this case the purpose of the operation would be to separate the twins and so give Jodie a reasonably good prospect of a long and reasonably normal life. Mary's death would not be the purpose of the operation, although it would be its inevitable consequence. The operation would give her, even in death, bodily integrity as a human being. She would die, not because she was intentionally killed, but because her body cannot sustain her life.

(vii) Continued life, whether long or short, would hold nothing for Mary except possible pain and discomfort, if indeed she can feel anything at all.

(viii) The proposed operation would therefore be in the best interests of each of the twins. The decision does not require the court to value one life above another.

(ix) The proposed operation would not be unlawful. It would involve the positive invasive surgery and Mary's death would be forseen as an inevitable consequence of an operation which is intended, and is necessary, to save Jodie's life. But Mary's death would not be the purpose or intention of the surgery, and she would die because tragically her body, on its own, is not and never has been viable'.

The Right to a Fair Trial

Article 6 provides that everyone has a right to a fair trial and by Article 6 (3) (c) it is provided that everyone may defend himself in person or through legal assistance of his own choosing or, if he has not sufficient means to pay for legal assistance, to be given it free when the interests of justice so require.

Article 13 states that 'Everyone whose rights and freedoms are set forth in this Convention shall have an effective remedy before a national authority notwithstanding that the violation has been committed by persons acting in an official capacity.' The Human Rights Act 1998 has not incorporated Article 13.

Public Funding

The Lord Chancellor is proposing a substantial cut in public funding. This may result in parents and children not receiving adequate legal representation. In *Airey* v. *Ireland*[136] a wife made an application to the European Court for breach of Article 13. She wished to bring High Court proceedings for a decree of judicial separation but lacked the means to employ a lawyer. The court found that in circumstances where the procedure was complex, there were complicated points of law, a need to call and examine expert witnesses and such emotional involvement of the parties that the possibility of the wife appearing in person before the High Court did not provide the wife with an effective right of access to the court. For the access to be effective, she required legal representation which would have to be publicly funded due to her limited finances.

A right to a fair hearing includes the principle of 'equality of arms', freedom from self-incrimination, access to evidence, presence in court, adversarial argument and reasons for judgment. The principle of equality of arms in family law has potential for making impact on the current practice of joint instructions relating to expert reports in child care cases where complex medical issues are involved. Articles 6 and 8 are likely to impact upon the High Court's view[137] that in all cases where the welfare of the child is the court's paramount consideration, there is a positive duty upon all parties and their legal advisers to make full and frank disclosure of all matters material to the welfare of the child whether favourable or adverse to their own case.

The refusal of legal aid for legal representation of children in proceedings under section 34 (4) has been the subject of a recent appeal[138]. The Legal Aid Board had refused the grant of legal aid on the basis that alternative funding was available under regulation 9 (1) Guardian ad litem and Reporting Officers (Panels) Regulations 1991 and that the Guardian's legal costs could be met by the Panel. Although the Court of Appeal agreed that regulation 9 (1) was widely enough construed to include the possibility that the Guardian ad litem be funded by the Guardian ad litem Panel, Lord Justice Thorpe stated he would construe 'reasonable expenses' literally and confine them to those directly incurred by the Guardian, namely those for which he was contractually liable to a third party. His Lordship expressed the hope that the Regulation 9 argument would not be used again by the Legal Services Commission to avoid the award of public funding to a child in similar circumstances.

Confidentiality of Parent's Evidence in Care Proceedings

Another problematic area concerns confidentiality of parent's evidence in care proceedings where criminal proceedings are pending. It has been argued

---

[136] *Airey* v. *Ireland* 2 EHRR 305.
[137] *Oxfordshire County Council* v. *P* [1995] Fam 161.
[138] *W and Others* v. *Legal Services Commission* [2000] 2 FLR 821.

that section 98 Children Act 1989[139] did not preclude a parent being cross-examined as to such statements or admissions in the criminal proceedings.

Article 6 has been held to require that a party be allowed to consult the relevant evidence which is available to the authorities, and to obtain the attendance and examination of witnesses on his behalf under the same conditions as witnesses against him. In *Hendriks* v. *The Netherlands*[140] where the applicant father in a contact case was allowed to read a report of the *Council for the Protection of Children* but not to keep a copy, the Commission did not exclude that such circumstances may prejudice an applicant's position before the court, so as to constitute a breach of Article 6.

Under Article 6 there is an implied right to give oral evidence and this may be relevant to cases where there currently is no oral evidence heard, for example child abduction cases and ex parte emergency protection orders. There may be an argument for more fully contested interim care orders which are presently frequently made without oral evidence.

In family cases time runs from the initiation of the court proceedings. Delay is acknowledged as detrimental by the Children Act 1989, section 1 (2) and will also be a breach of Article 6.

Right to a Public Hearing

The current practice of hearing children's cases in private has been considered by the Court of Appeal in the light of Article 6[141]. Lord Justice Butler-Sloss said '. . . it would seem to me that the present procedures in family proceedings are in accordance with the spirit of the Convention'. The question of whether judgement should be given publicly in children's cases has been left for the future[142].

Leave for Party Status

The Convention rights of parties should be taken into account in applications for leave for party status where one party will suffer detriment as a result of another being granted party status. Section 10 (9) of the Children Act sets out matters for consideration when considering applications for party status in private law proceedings but there is no similar provision for applications by the unmarried father for party status in care proceedings.

---

[139] S 98(2), a statement of admission made in such proceedings shall not be admissable in evidence against the person making it or his spouse in proceedings for an offence other than perjury.
[140] *Hendriks* v. *Netherlands* 5 EHRR 223, *Feldbrugge* v. *The Netherlands* 8 EHRR 425.
[141] *Re PB (Hearings in Open Court)* 2 [1996] 2 FLR 765.
[142] *Re PB* supra 770F.

Leave for Custodial Parent to Remove Child from the Jurisdiction

Where leave is sought for the custodial parent to remove a child from the jurisdiction resulting in a dramatic reduction in contact between the child and the non-custodial parent, there will be a need to balance The convention rights of each party, including the child (Article 8). In *Re A*[143], the Court of Appeal found that while Article 8 undoubtedly gave the father and the child a right to family life, Article 8 (1) gave the mother a right to a private life and Article 8 (2) required the court to balance such rights when they were in conflict. The test set out in the authorities, that, if the custodial parent were taking a reasonable decision, the court ordinarily should not interfere with that decision unless there was some compelling reason in the child's best interests to the contrary, was not in conflict with the Convention.

Leave to Withdraw Application for Care Order

Where care proceedings have been issued and leave is sought to withdraw the proceedings it has been held[144] there was nothing in the European Convention which required the court to act otherwise than in the interests of the child. Due to previous difficulties with the parents' four older children, the local authority sought an Emergency Protection Order and commenced care proceedings following the birth of their fifth child. A psychiatric assessment of both parents demonstrated that their care of the baby was exemplary and concluded the baby should remain with them. The local authority applied to withdraw the proceedings and the parents supported the application relying inter alia upon Article 8.

The Guardian ad litem opposed the withdrawal of the proceedings on the basis that the local authority's investigations had failed to take account of the wealth of evidence in respect of the four older children, and the failure of the parents to accept or co-operate with assistance and advice given to them by social services, the educational authorities and medical experts. The court refused to grant leave to withdraw as the Guardian ad litem had advanced solid and cogent reasons, despite the views of the local authority, to support her view that there was a pressing social need for state intervention to protect this baby in the future. The case should proceed to hearing as time-tabled for the contentious evidence to be heard and ruled upon.

---

[143] *Re A* [2000] 2 FLR 225.
[144] *Re N* [2000] 1 FLR 134.

Interplay Between Article 9 and Section 2 (7) Children Act 1989

The interplay between section 2 (7) Children Act 1989[145] and Article 9, dealing with freedom of thought, conscience and religion, has been dealt with by the Court of Appeal[146]. Here the father applied for a specific issue order for his son to be circumcised. He was a practising Muslim and the mother a non-practising Christian. It was held circumcision falls within a small group of decisions made on behalf of a child which, in the absence of agreement of those with parental responsibility, ought not to be carried out or arranged notwithstanding section 2 (7) Children Act 1989. Lord Justice Butler-Sloss stated that '. . . the decision to circumcise on a ground other than medical necessity is a very important one; the operation is irreversible and should only be carried out where the parents together approve of it, or in the absence of parental agreement, where the court decides that the operation is in the best interests of the child'. The Court stated that in a similar category would be decisions in respect of sterilisation, and change of surname.

Conclusion

In practical terms the main Convention Rights being incorporated into domestic law will provide a further basis of argument in support of a party's stance, whether the child or the parent. Convention points will be arguable at all levels from the outset. It may provide the means to justify an order sought, for example an assessment under section 38 (6) where the local authority do not propose to assess a parent, and the care plan is for immediate placement with an alternative family. Conversely it may provide the means to oppose an order, for example where the care plan will mean the separation of siblings[147], or where a supervision order would provide the child with adequate protection and the local authority are seeking a care order. Where a person believes that he is a 'victim' of a breach of Convention rights and the court fails to take account of that party's Convention rights it may constitute a ground of appeal to a higher court, and ultimately to the European Court of Justice. The practitioner must continually be aware of the need to take account of each party's Convention rights and the need to carry out the balancing exercise.

---

[145]'Where more than one person has parental responsibility for a child, each of them may act alone and without the other (or others) in meeting that responsibility; but nothing in this Part shall be taken to affect the operation of any enactment which requires the consent of more than one person in a matter affecting the child'.
[146] *Re J (Specific Issue Orders)* [2000] 1 FLR 571.
[147] *Johansen* v. *Norway* (1996) 23 EHRR, 67 at 64.

11 The Way Forward: CAFCASS and the Future for the Representation of Children in Family Proceedings

Arran Poyser

Introduction

The views expressed in this chapter are those of the writer and not necessarily those of the Department of Health or the Lord Chancellor's Department.

Such is the pace of development within CAFCASS preparation that, at the time this Chapter is being written early in 2001, it risks in some respects being out of date before publication. Regardless of the April 2001 commencement deadline for CAFCASS, this is a useful opportunity to take stock on some important issues. Having set out in summary the contextual background, the selection of themes in the first part of this Chapter discusses what may be on the CAFCASS agenda for the way forward. The Chapter concludes with an overview of some of the key issues about the representation of children in family proceedings.

CAFCASS

The main stages in the timetable to establish CAFCASS may be summarised as follows:

- **May 1997.** General Election and change of Government.
- **June 1997.** Comprehensive Spending Review (CSR) across Government Departments.
- **Autumn 1997.** Officials from Government Departments (Lord Chancellor's Department, Home Office, Department of Health) prepared a paper for Ministers suggesting that integrating current court welfare services into a new unified service would be worth exploring fully by way of consultation.
- **February 1998.** Ministers announced that further detailed work involving practitioners and other users of the service should be undertaken to form the basis for public consultation.
- **March-May 1998.** Three meetings of a Working Group took place to prepare consultation paper.

- **July 1998.** Consultation paper *Support Services in Family Proceedings: Future Organisation of Court Welfare Services* published.
- **November 1998.** At close of consultation over 300 responses had been received.
- **July 1999.** Ministers announced that, when legislation allowed, a new unified service would be established across England and Wales; the Lord Chancellor would take the lead responsibility and set up an implementation team; the new body would be a Non-Departmental Public Body (NDPB).
- **November 1999.** Legislation included in the new Parliamentary Session.
- **March 2000.** Criminal Justice and Court Services Bill published and started its Parliamentary process.
- **October 2000.** Chairman of Board appointed.
- **November 2000.** Members of Board appointed (10) but details not announced publicly until 2001.
- **November 2000.** 10 Regional Manager posts and 10 Business Unit Manager posts advertised.
- **30 November 2000.** Bill completed in Parliament and received Royal Assent.
- **December 2000.** Chief Executive appointed.
- **December 2000-January 2001.** Head of Finance, Head of Human Resources and Head of Legal Services appointed.
- **February 2001.** First Board Meeting.

Preparing for CAFCASS

Preparing for any organisational change is complex. A new managerial specialism called 'change management' is very much in evidence. Each organisational change is unique but may often have particular features in common. Special factors influencing how CAFCASS should be established include the following:

- About 2000 staff across England and Wales to be moved into CAFCASS within the 17 month period from the announcement that there would be a Bill to the date the service is established.
- Securing transfer budgets from current services to CAFCASS and start-up funding to cover implementation project and investment in IT.
- Managing primary and secondary legislation.
- Minimum disruption of services to courts, children and families.
- Part of the change affecting family court welfare to be co-ordinated with a parallel re-organisation within the same time-scale and under the same legislation to establish the National Probation Service (NPS).
- Ensuring wide consultation and involvement of all staff in the change process.
- Consulting fully throughout with courts, the legal professions, users of services.

- Consulting widely with voluntary organisations who are contracted and funded to provide services such as mediation or guardian ad litem services.
- Evolving authority and responsibility regarding decision-making, involving the:
  - —current service providers and the four government department sponsors (Welsh Office initially, then Welsh Assembly, Lord Chancellor's Department, Home Office and Department of Health)
  - —project team
  - —chair of the board
  - —board members
  - —chief executive
  - —senior managers
- Harmonising current salaries and self-employment issues.

Court Rules

An important area of secondary legislation supporting the establishment of CAFCASS is contained in the proposed revised family proceedings rules and adoption rules. The scope of the revision addresses the following objectives:

- To make any necessary legal amendments to current court rules resulting from the establishment of CAFCASS and consequential repeals and amendments carried in the Criminal Justice and Court Services Act 2000 (CJCSA 2000).
- To take the opportunity for limited improvements and related clarifications in the light of a number of years of operational experience.
- To ensure where possible consistency between the powers and duties of officers of the service when appointed in any family or related proceedings.
- To amend court forms as necessary.

References to guardians ad litem, reporting officers and probation officers are subsumed within the Criminal Justice and Court Services Act as 'officers of the service'. Before April 2001, the relevant court rules refer to welfare officers, guardians ad litem, reporting officers and the Official Solicitor. These will mainly be replaced by new names covering the different professional duties undertaken by officers. Table 1 summarises the position.

The issue of names was highly sensitive, more so within the current services than with the public at large. There was little consensus about names within the CAFCASS project, among the advisory groups or across the services more generally. The new names were incorporated into the amendment rules. At the end of the day, it might be argued that service users probably care a great deal more about the quality of service they receive than the name of the person providing that service. It is likely that within CAFCASS a generic name may be adopted for front-line workers although it will not be a statutory title.

Table 1: Professional names

Current name	New name after 1 April 2001
• Guardian ad litem (Children Act 1989: care related and secure accommodation)	Children's guardian
• Welfare officer (Children Act section 7 (where undertaken by CAFCASS)	Children and family reporter
• Welfare officer (Children Act section 7 (where undertaken by a local authority)	Welfare officer
• Guardian ad litem (Adoption Act 1976: adoption and freeing)	Children's guardian
• Reporting Officer (Adoption Act 1976: adoption and freeing)	Reporting officer
• Guardian ad litem (Human Fertilisation and Embryology Act (parental orders)	Parental order reporter

Within CAFCASS, officers, as with current services, will undertake a range of cases some of which will be complex and most involving crucial decisions by courts about the welfare of children. In advising courts on these issues and, usually, preparing reports for final hearings, a modern service needs to ensure that its authority for undertaking this work is clearly understood by the public and by other professionals working across the family justice system. Public understanding may be enhanced by a range of CAFCASS information leaflets to address these and related needs.

A further source of professional authority is derived from setting out powers and duties of officers within a statutory framework of regulation or court rules. All the principal functions of officers of the service in relation to court proceedings are now set out in such rules. This translates the principle, already well-established in Children Act public law and Adoption related proceedings, to Children Act private law cases. The rule changes therefore include private law (Section 7) reporting undertaken by officers of CAFCASS.

The proposed amendment rules substitute a new rule 4.11 for that in the 1991 Rules. This deals with the general powers and duties of officers of the service, whether appointed as the children's guardian or the children and family reporter. Formerly, these powers and duties were restricted to the guardian ad litem. These general powers and duties include:

- Having regard to the welfare principle and welfare checklist set out in Section 1 of the Children Act.
- Making such investigations as may be necessary.
- Contacting and seeking to interview such persons as he thinks appropriate or the court directs.
- Obtaining such professional assistance as is available to him which he thinks appropriate or which the court directs him to obtain.
- Assisting the court in any other way that it might require under this rule or Rules 4.11A and 4.11B.

- Being available to be questioned by a party about his oral or written evidence.

Although the above powers and duties have not been part of the rules for the conduct of Section 7 enquiries by probation officers, they reflect common good practice. These general powers and duties are supplemented by additional powers and duties. These cover either the children's guardian or the children and family reporter and are set out below. In respect of the children's guardian, the proposed changes are minimal because they are fully set out in the 1991 rules.

The amendment rules also propose an insert of a new Rule 4.11B setting out the additional powers and duties of a children and family reporter. This rule requires the children and family reporter:

- To notify the child of the contents of his report as he considers appropriate to the age and understanding of the child, including any reference to the child's own views on the application and the reporter's recommendation.
- If he does notify the child of any contents of his report, to explain them to the child in a manner appropriate to his age and understanding.
- To advise the court if he considers that another person should, in safeguarding the interests of the child, be made a party.
- To consider whether the child should be made a party to the proceedings.
- To notify the court if he considers the child should be made a party together with his reasons.
- If the court directs, to attend any hearing at which his report is to be considered.

The new rules also cover certain children cases currently handled by the Official Solicitor (OS). The role of the Official Solicitor is to provide confidential advice to civil courts and to represent minors where there are issues of legal or moral complexity central to their welfare. Functions are similar to, but not identical with, those of a guardian ad litem in specified proceedings under Section 41 of the Children Act 1989 and in child related proceedings to act as the child's solicitor. Under CAFCASS, this work will be dealt with by specialist caseworkers and in-house lawyers transferred across from the children's side of the OS. Their appointment will continue to be restricted to the higher courts and is expected to be covered by updated guidance from CAFCASS with the agreement of the President of the Family Division.

European Convention on Human Rights (ECHR)

The ECHR was incorporated into United Kingdom law in October 2000. Although Britain helped draft the Convention more than 50 years ago, British Citizens could not have access to its protection directly through British courts. Instead, they had to take the issue to the European Court at Strasbourg, but only having first exhausted their legal remedies in the British courts. This was expensive and took many years. The Human Rights Act 1998 changes this and much more. Many have ambitions for the positive effect the Act will have on the way the rights of adults as well as those of children are thought about. They argue that, over time, there will be a real change in culture. They hope for a greater understanding about, and respect for, human rights. There will be those who may wish to take up challenges through the courts, alleging that their human rights have been infringed. It seems likely that although many may fail, some may succeed. A number of articles of the Convention are particularly relevant to family law and therefore to CAFCASS. Examples of these include:

• The right to life (Article 2).
• Protection from torture and inhuman degrading treatment or punishment (Article 3).
• The right to liberty and security of the person (Article 5).
• The right to a fair trial (Article 6).
• Protection of private and family life (Article 8).
• The right to freedom of expression (Article 10).
• The right to marry and found a family (Article 12).
• Freedom from discrimination in the delivery of Convention rights (Article 14).

Professional practice may have to change to ensure full compliance with the Act. Some organisations may be persuaded to do so if, for example, they are publicly criticised. Courts have considerable powers to impose financial penalties on public organisations that breach the Convention. For CAFCASS, officers of the service may, for example, have to pay more attention to ensuring that relevant parties are given full explanations, perhaps backed up with written information, as to role of CAFCASS in the proceedings.

The approach taken in planning CAFCASS has been to ensure that rules of court setting out the powers and duties of officers of CAFCASS are framed with ECHR in mind. As a public body, CAFCASS has to have due regard to the implications of the Human Rights Act. Much work that is to be undertaken in CAFCASS involves issues concerning private and family life. This work falls within scope of the qualified rights set out in Article 8 of the Convention. Any such potential breaches may be justified under the provisions of Article 8 (2):

> *8 (2) There shall be no interference by a public body with the exercise of this right excepts such as in accordance with the law and is necessary in a democratic society in the interests of national security, public safety or the economic well-being of the country, for the prevention of disorder or crime, for the protection of health or morals, or for the protection of the rights and freedoms of others.*

Setting out the principal powers and duties of officers of CAFCASS in court rules helps satisfy an important element of this Article concerning the words quoted above, particularly 'in accordance with the law'. Although there is some anxiety that in balancing parents rights and children's welfare, the focus on the child might be lost, the case-law from the European Court in Strasbourg places great emphasis on importance of the child's welfare, as can be seen in the preceding chapter. This would seem to suggest that the Children Act 1989 continues to provide a sound framework for good practice.

The United Nations Convention on the Rights of the Child (UNCRC)

The United Kingdom ratified UNCRC in 1991. It is the most supported of all UN conventions with over 190 countries world wide having ratified. However, unlike the ECHR, its provision cannot be enforced through the courts unless individual countries have incorporated its provisions into their domestic legislation. Britain has not done so although there are a very few occasions where legislation has been drafted with the Convention in mind: the Children (Scotland) Act 1995 is a notable example. Apart from some very articulate academics and specialist children's rights groups, UNCRC has a rather low profile in the UK. It is not generally used as a working document to help frame our policies or day to day practices. Copies of the Convention are not usually in evidence on the desks of officials, ready to be consulted daily. Against this rather negative picture, note should be taken of some very imaginative examples of working with school children of all ages around the key Convention Articles, as part of a developing curriculum around citizenship. Some of this work has been taken forward by voluntary organisations such as 'Save the Children Fund', with some central government funding.

One or two of the Articles on UNCRC have taken a wider hold. For example, Article 12 has particular importance for the work of CAFCASS:

12 (1) States Parties shall assure to the child who is capable of forming his or her own views the right to express those views freely in all matters affecting the child, the views of the child being given due weight in accordance with the age and maturity of the child.

12 (2) For this purpose, the child shall in particular be provided the opportunity to be heard in any judicial and administrative proceedings affecting the child, either directly, or through a representative or an appropriate body, in a manner consistent with the procedural rules of national law.

The Views of Service Users

For a number of reasons, the voice of the child has been given far greater emphasis over the last few years and there are major social welfare programmes and Government driven initiatives around child participation. Listening to the child, an integral concept of good social work practice, has been both lost and rediscovered in the last decade. The Tribunal of Inquiry into Abuse in North Wales *Lost in Care* (2000) is an example of a low point and the Government's programme of improving services for looked after children (*Quality Protects*) has a particular emphasis on child participation. These developments should be considered against the wider programme of reforms which *Learning the Lessons* (2000) outlines as the Government response to *Lost in Care*. Client power on behalf of a range of particular interest groups has emerged more strongly in social welfare. It can also be seen as part of a wider consumer protection movement and as series of campaigns with well-organised access to the media and to Parliament.

Within CAFCASS, there has been wide consultation with groups who represent fathers' interests in divorce, child residence and child contact matters, women's groups concerned about domestic violence, and children's groups (but not children directly).

Working with such organisations is a challenge. They often have high ambitions and expectations as to what should be done and what is achievable. They may at times be highly critical of the standards of current services. They may dismiss official explanations or points of view. Although the fathers' and mothers' groups all claim to wish to put the welfare of children first, they tend to differ in their analysis of the underlying causes of any problems and therefore the direction in which solutions might be found. Whilst some might be characterised as 'anti-professional', others are well-informed and set out to work in partnership with the relevant central government authorities. CAFCASS will need to develop good contacts with these organisations and interests, reflecting Government policy to engage more closely with the consumer. CAFCASS will also need to give careful thought to its links with the media, given that most of its work is governed by strict rules of confidentiality. In short, although CAFCASS may well have a good story to tell: it must find legitimate ways of being able to tell it. Of particular importance is to ensure that close contact with mothers' and fathers' groups does not deflect from a need for CAFCASS to remain child-focussed.

Inspection and Quality Assurance

One reason for establishing CAFCASS was to achieve better consistency of service quality provision around the country. It was decided that inspection should form an important element in monitoring quality and performance. Section 17 of the Criminal Justice and Court Services Act requires the Magistrates' Courts Service Inspectorate (MCSI) to undertake that inspection. A new unit has been established within MCSI to develop and staff an inspection programme.

MCSI has adopted the following guiding principles to govern the way it works. These are likely to be applicable to CAFCASS inspection work. MCSI will:

- Exercise independence of judgement.
- Treat people courteously and fairly and in a non discriminatory way.

- Work in a non adversarial way.
- Have regard to the demands it makes on those being inspected.
- Be open about its practices, procedures and the expectations against which inspection judgements are made.
- Monitor and evaluate its performance.
- Respond constructively to any suggestions or complaints about the way it goes about its work.

No decisions have yet been made about the details of the inspection programme or the methodologies that will be used. It is likely that inspection work will be supported by a protocol designed to assist staff in both MCSI and CAFCASS to establish a clear and effective working relationship. These kind of arrangements may also need to address the interface between MCSI and the Lord Chancellor's Department (LCD) and take account of LCD's monitoring responsibilities for CAFCASS.

The internal structures within CAFCASS for dealing effectively with quality assurance issues have only recently been finalised. It is expected that the Lord Chancellor in exercising his powers of direction under CJCSA 2000 will require CAFCASS to publish National Standards. Preliminary work including some consultation on a draft framework has already taken place. Discussion about the scope and structure of any such standards, the intended audience, their relationship with performance indicators and other service related targets will need resolution before publication.

Performance and Outcomes

Another significant development in recent years is the emphasis on public organisations having clear measures of performance and of outcomes. Linked to National Standards, it is likely that there will be a set of performance measures covering the main aspects of CAFCASS. These may include front line practice, administration and management. These performance measures may well be developed quickly and might in part form an element of the contract (similar to a public service agreement) between the CAFCASS Board and the LCD Minister with overall responsibility for CAFCASS and accountability to Parliament.

The civil and criminal justice systems have been and continue to be the subject of reviews that have sought to set clear objectives and frameworks for the effective handling of business on an inter-agency basis. Examples include the legal profession, the courts in civil and criminal work, the police, and the Crown Prosecution Service. However, there has been no equivalent action taken for family work. Outcomes, targets and other similar concepts have not been set by Government for the family justice system. This poses a particular challenge for CAFCASS at the heart of family work. The present position is that agencies are seen working to different masters and to different objectives. There is no overall measurement of the effectiveness of the system. There is no clarity over roles and responsibilities. It is not

possible to set clear performance standards and benchmark future improvements without a proper framework for family justice in which roles and
responsibilities are clearly defined and owned. These are the kind of issues
that are now being given serious attention within the senior Civil Service.

Monitoring and Research

CAFCASS is investing heavily in information technology (IT). This should
facilitate a considerable level of monitoring about the service and, in
particular, the court proceedings that form such a large element of its
workload. IT will also service financial and personnel functions. Designing
the IT requires clarity on many questions including:

• Which aspects of CAFCASS need to be monitored?
• What information needs to be collected?
• Who needs what information, how often and why?
• Is information collection maximising its potential?

Research is invaluable providing that it is well conducted and addresses policy
or practice issues likely to be of value to the wider world. But research can
often taken several years to complete by which time the policy or practice
agenda has moved on. CAFCASS will no doubt wish to consider developing a
research strategy. Early dilemmas may include setting out a rational approach
for the distribution of scarce research funding. What may be less acceptable,
for example, is the payment of significant sums to researchers for them to
collect the basic data that CAFCASS ought to be routinely collecting though
its national and local monitoring. This kind of issue has reportedly occurred
in respect of some research into GALRO and family court welfare during the
1990s. CAFCASS has arranged meetings with many of the country's leading
researchers in this area to help inform its research strategic thinking.

Influencing Wider Family Policy and Practice

Good research clearly has influenced Government thinking in the broad area
of family policy as well as best practice. It is reasonable to expect that to
continue. CAFCASS, as a national body across England and Wales, should
be in a position to speak authoritatively on family policy and practice issues
of concern to Government. In that sense, CAFCASS will be 'at the top
table'. It should use that potential influence wisely and it may well need to
have the capacity to draw on high quality information and research
generated within its service. At the same time, making research findings
easily available to practitioners though IT is of obvious importance.

Continuing Professional Development

The main principle that CAFCASS is committed to support is to ensure that
whenever officers of CAFCASS are appointed to advise courts, they have

the training, skills and experience relevant to those proceedings; and that management and administration within CAFCASS serve to support this aim.

Any discussion about professional training within CAFCASS needs to be placed within the wider context of developments around social work training. Plans for the Diploma in Social Work (DipSW) highlight that the situation is very fluid and, as such, there are many uncertainties. The Diploma is not considered sufficiently detailed to equip those completing it to undertake many social work tasks. For example, the Department of Health (DH) has supported the development of the PQ Child Care Award which all child care workers in social services department will be expected to have by 2005. It is currently being piloted by a number of academic providers with a wide range of authorities.

In 2000, DH issued the JM Consulting report on critical DipSW options and how reform should proceed. A consultation paper *A Quality Strategy for Social Care* sought views, among other issues, on the way fo. ward for the reform of social work education; how post-qualification training might be developed in the future; and how best to recruit and retain professional social workers.

There are a range of important Government initiatives, such as the Department of Health Quality Protects programme and the Department for Education and Employment (DfEE) led Connexions Service, which are adding to current pressures regarding the recruitment of workers with a DipSW. This shortage was graphically described by the Chief Inspector of Social Services in her 10th Annual Report:

> *During the year councils have reported to us that they are having the utmost difficulty recruiting competent staff to fill posts which are critical to the delivery of the government's agenda. This recruitment shortage raises a number of issues, which need resolution if services are to improve. Firstly, people who seek employment following the award of the Diploma in Social Work are said not to have the experience, skill and knowledge necessary to do the job. Secondly, too many people who have been working in social care services for some time and who are applying for a specialist or more senior post are said not to have the competence required. Thirdly, there do not appear to be enough people working in the service, many posts in social care offer less pay than less demanding jobs in supermarkets. Fourthly, government programmes for example, the expansions in youth services, inspection and regulation of care services, and children's services have expanded the demand for people with similar experience and knowledge without the equivalent expansion of supply.*

CAFCASS activities are not seen as suitable for new social work graduates. Instead the organisation is likely to need to rely on those who are both well qualified and experienced. CAFCASS will need to out-compete in a highly competitive market. There is no social work training at either a basic level or an advanced level such as a Masters degree that focuses on CAFCASS alone. Initial discussions with a range of universities have explored the practicalities of developing a Masters programme. No major obstacles have been identified. This kind of programme cannot be achieved overnight but may hopefully be taken forward by CAFCASS as one of its medium term aims.

There is also need to invest in the continuous professional development of all CAFCASS staff and such an approach requires both funding and a change of culture. The cultural change is to establish CAFCASS as a 'learning agency' which has been defined as 'an organisation that demonstrably takes an integrated and co-ordinated approach to training and related issues, such as practice and evidence based research, appraisal and continuing development of all staff'.

Careful thought is needed about the range of subjects around which learning should be concentrated, as well as the best ways of delivering learning programmes.

The Nature of Professional Advice in Family Court Work

CAFCASS officers are likely to have great influence on the ways courts reach decisions about children in difficult circumstances. Much of that advice is about predicting the future. It is about assessing risks. It involves making careful judgements concerning family strengths and weaknesses as well as how best to promote both the short-term and long-term interests of children. Courts rely heavily on the expertise of the services that will make up CAFCASS.

But for reasons already mentioned earlier in this chapter concerning the rights of service users, the officer's judgement must be soundly based. Both the Act setting up CAFCASS and the revised court rules allow for the cross-examination in court of the officer. This might well cover the conclusions reached, the reasons underlying those conclusions and, of course, the recommendations. That is a considerable challenge when much of what is recommended may be perceived by some as being based on 'belief', 'custom and practice' or 'conventional wisdom'. An ever more professionally disciplined approach, including where appropriate use of a thorough research evidenced argument, may be required.

Development of Court Diversion Options

In Britain, the family justice system costs many millions of pounds annually. Services that support orders after court such as contact centres, or before court such as mediation are sometimes described as being very short of resources. The balance of where resources are directed may need further serious consideration. Some of the issues are uncomfortable. For example, is it reasonable for the State to underpin financially lengthy and painful in-court disputes about contact and residence where separating parents are unable to reach agreement?

CAFCASS may provide a much-needed stimulus to develop further models of pre-court dispute resolution suitable for family work, perhaps for example, adapting work around formal pre-court meetings in child protection, that has been developed in certain Australian jurisdictions, such as New South Wales and Victoria. Nearer to hand in Europe, there may much more to be learned about using courts as one of the last options rather than one of the first.

The Representation of Children in Family Proceedings

The 1998 Consultation Paper

The second part of this Chapter explores aspects of the debate about the representation of children in family proceedings. This issue was included as Chapter 4 of the 1998 Consultation Paper *Support Services in Family Proceedings: Future Organisation of Court Welfare Services*. It should be noted that this topic was not strictly within the terms of reference for the consultation paper announced by the Government in February 1998. A valuable survey around this topic undertaken by a senior Family Division Judge in 1997, elicited a large number of detailed responses from across professional groups concerned with these matters. It was considered appropriate to take this work forward by posing key questions to a wider audience. This then formed Chapter 4 of the Consultation Paper. The questions were as follows:

Q16. Within a new unified service, should limited discretion be introduced as to the use of legal representation for children in public law cases? If it is, what should be the scope of any flexibility and who should exercise it?

Q17. Within a new unified service, are there types of private law cases in which a wider range of welfare duties should be undertaken by caseworkers? In what circumstances might it be appropriate for a child to be joined as a party to private law proceedings and entitled to separate legal representation? Should this be possible in the family proceedings court as well as in the higher courts?

Q18. Should the Government implement Section 64 of the Family Law Act 1996? If so, should this proceed independently of the Government's consideration of proposals to set up a unified court welfare service? Should rules define the criteria for separate representation by a court welfare officer, by a legal representative and by both?

Q19. Is the suggested range of functions for an in-house legal capacity within a new, integrated court welfare service appropriate?

Q20. In what circumstances, if at all, would it be appropriate for children to be represented by in-house lawyers from the service?

Q21. In cases where external legal representation is needed, should children always be represented by solicitors and/or barristers who are able to demonstrate specialist knowledge and experience through some form of accreditation similar to that of the Law Society Children's Panel? Are the proposals likely to ensure improved control of legal costs and consistent quality of legal representation?

However, the responses to these questions did bear directly on the Government's decision to proceed towards a unified court welfare service. The issues continued to be discussed and have informed key areas of decision-making about how CAFCASS will operate.

The funding code and the 'tandem model'

There is likely to be very little change in practice in the area of the representation of children following the establishment of CAFCASS. The Community Legal Services (CLS) Funding Code does not breach the basic principle of State funded legal representation for children in public law applications. During the passage of the Criminal Justice and Court Services Bill, Ministers repeatedly emphasised that the 'tandem model' of guardian and child's legal representative was not under threat.

Adoption

In adoption related proceedings, the Prime Minister's Review on Adoption (July 2000) and the White Paper *Adoption: a new approach* (December 2000) have not addressed the issues of the child becoming a party to the proceedings with legal representation. This will continue to be allowed where a clear need is established and the court authorises party status for the child.

Child as a party in private proceedings

There has been no decisive shift in thinking as to when, in private law (typically, contested section 8 applications around residence and contact) the child should be joined as a party and, as such, be entitled to legal representation. It appears this will continue to be judged on a case-by-case basis with due regard to any legal precedents.

The proposed family proceedings amendment rules do, however, make it an explicit duty for the CAFCASS officer to consider the child's party status. The amendment rules insert a new Rule 4.11B setting out the additional powers and duties of a children and family reporter. This rule, amongst other matters, requires the children and family reporter:

- To consider whether the child should be made a party to the proceedings.
- To notify the court if he considers the child should be made a party together with his reasons.

Another of the amendment rules amends Rule 4.13 of the 1991 Rules by clarifying at paragraph (1) that the reference to welfare officer is in accordance with Section 7(1)(b): that is the power of the court to request a report from a local authority. After paragraph (3) paragraphs (3A) and (3B) are inserted, and these require the welfare officer to consider whether the child should be made a party to the proceedings and, if he does, to advise the court of this and his reasons.

The discretion for the court to make the child a party is not reserved to the higher courts. However, the family proceedings court may, for reasons of complexity or on other grounds, elect to transfer the case up.

Separate representation: the Section 64 provisions
In January 2001, the Lord Chancellor announced to Parliament that the Government was not satisfied that it would be right to proceed with the implementation of Part II of the Family Law Act 1996. Parliament would be invited to repeal the relevant sections of the Act, once a suitable legislative opportunity occurred. The provisions for separate representation for children set out in Part IV at Section 64 remain on the statute book but it appears that there is no active consideration as to bringing this section into force. The section gives the Lord Chancellor a discretionary power to make regulations for the separate representation of children in proceedings which relate to any matter in respect of which a question has arisen, or may arise, under Part II of the Act; Part IV of the Act; (Family Homes and Domestic Violence already implemented) and Acts of 1973 and 1978.

Involving the child without party status
The proposed family proceedings amendment rules clarify further the powers and duties of CAFCASS officers both in private law (Section 7) and in public law reporting under the Children Act 1989. But these issues do not deal with the representation of children as such although they do promote better practice regarding the involvement of the child.

For example, the proposed Rule 4.11A sets out the additional powers and duties of the children's guardian. These include ensuring that, in relation to a decision made by the court in the proceedings, if he considers it appropriate to the age and understanding of the child, the child is notified of that decision and, if the child is notified, in a manner appropriate to his age and understanding.

This new provision is aimed at ensuring that the issue of notifying the child of a court decision is actively considered. The rule does not necessarily require the children's guardian to notify the child in any particular case. Depending on the circumstances, a more appropriate person may be identified. But is it desirable that all the relevant persons (including the child) and the court are aware of the proposed arrangements to notify the child.

The proposed amendment rules also insert new Rule 4.11B requirements that include that the children and family reporter must notify the child of the contents of his report as he considers appropriate to the age and understanding of the child, including any reference to the child's own views on the application and the reporter's recommendation.

If he does notify the child of any contents of his report, he must explain them to the child in a manner appropriate to his age and understanding.

There is no equivalent duty of the children and family reporter to ensure that the child is notified of court decisions but it is hoped that courts and practitioners will examine best approaches in this area and also involve the child's parents, as far as is possible.

The children's work of the Official Solicitor
As has already been mentioned, within CAFCASS the former children's work of the Official Solicitor (OS) transfers to a specialist central unit. The proposed court rules reflect these changes. Clause 15 of the Criminal Justice and Court Services Bill sought to ensure that this new position was reflected in the legislation. However, the wording of the clause was seen by some commentators as too broad and, they feared, might lead to a dismantling of the 'tandem model'. The Bill was therefore amended by the Government shortly before concluding its Parliamentary passage.

The arrangements for children's work formerly undertaken by the Official Solicitor and transferred to CAFCASS come under The Children and Family Court Advisory and Support Service (Officers Authorised to Conduct Litigation and Exercise Rights of Audience) Regulations 2001. These regulations are made under Section 15 of the Criminal Justice and Court Services Act 2000. They set out the prescribed description of an officer of the service conducting litigation and exercising a right of audience in proceedings. The regulations do not affect the generality of the guardian/solicitor 'tandem model' in public law.

Legal representation
The source of most children's legal representation under CAFCASS will continue to be accredited solicitors on local Law Society or equivalent panels. CAFCASS in-house legal representation will be restricted to the specialist central unit undertaking former OS children's work. The extent to which Law Society panels remain viable, given concerns about fee levels, franchising and related issues, will no doubt be closely monitored. But these matters essentially fall under the general remit of Community Legal Services and as such are well outside the service responsibilities of CAFCASS as set out in CJCSA 2000.

The duty on the children's guardian to appoint the solicitor for the child remains unchanged in the court rules. This policy was widely discussed but alternative suggestions, such as the selection of a child's solicitor by CAFCASS management or the courts, were firmly rejected. It is likely that all children's guardians will have to continue another aspect of current practice by demonstrating their use of an appropriate range of solicitors.

Non-legal representation
A further issue that has received some attention is whether there is a convincing argument for the child to have a non-legal representative in certain private and public law proceedings. Suggestions have been made that this might be some kind of advocate, solely concerned with ensuring that the

child's wishes are fully advanced in the proceedings. As such, the role would be unencumbered with statutory responsibilities of enquiry, advising on child welfare concerns and reporting to court. A number of questions seem central to this debate. For example, in what kinds of proceedings might such a person have most value for the child? Could such a service for children be established within the current legislative framework? How would such a service be funded and organised?

Conclusions

This Chapter shows that although there are a wide number of issues and influences impacting on the development of CAFCASS, the approach espoused of 'evolution rather than revolution' suggests that dramatic changes in policy and practice are unlikely. An evolutionary approach should also be able to embrace relevant concepts such as *Best Value* and continuous improvement in performance within a CAFCASS strategy and any Public Service Agreement between it and the Lord Chancellor's Department.

Conference commentators who have linked the establishment of CAF-CASS to doom-laden predictions that the representation of children in family proceedings is about to suffer a downward spiral to oblivion may find that their prophecies are very wide of the mark.

Two major jurisdictional and procedural court reviews have been undertaken in recent times. These are the Woolf report on civil proceedings *Access to Justice* (1996) and Lord Justice Auld's *Criminal Courts Review* (2001). What has not yet been covered is family proceedings work. This raises an important question as to whether family work should be a priority for such a comprehensive review.

References

ABSWAP (1983) *Black Children in Care: Evidence to the House of Commons Social Services Committee.* Association of Black Social Workers and Allied Professionals.

Alderson, P. (1993) *Children's Consent to Surgery.* Open University Press.

BAAF (1991) *Recruiting Black Families.* Practice Note 18. London, BAAF.

BAAF (1995) *The Placement Needs of Black Children.* Practice Note 13, London, BAAF.

Bagley, C. (1993) Trans-racial Adoption in Britain: A Follow up Study with Policy Considerations. *Child Welfare.* 72 (3).

Bagley, C. and Young, (1993) Colour it with Love. *Community Care.* February 28.

Bamford, F. and Wolkind, S. (1988) *The Physical and Mental Health Needs of Children in Care: Research Needs,* Two discussion papers, ESRC.

Barn, R. (Ed.) (1999) *Working with Black Children and Adolescents in Need.* London, BAAF.

Barn, R. *et al.* (1997) *Acting on Principle: An Examination of Race and Ethnicity in Social Services Provision for Children And Families.* London, BAAF.

Bebbington, A. and Miles, J. (1989) The Background of Children who Enter Local Authority Care, *British Journal of Social Work.* 19: 5.

Booth, Dame M. (1996) *Avoiding Delay in Children Act Cases.* DBE.

Brophy, J. (2000) Race and Ethnicity in Care Proceedings: Implications from a National Survey of Cases Containing Expert Evidence. *Adoption and Fostering.* 24: 2.

Brophy, Wale and Bates (1999) *Myths and Practices.* BAAF.

Clarke, A. and Sinclair, R. (1999). *The Child in Focus: The Evolving Role of the Guardian ad litem.* National Children's Bureau.

Clarke, D. (1995) *Whose Case is it Anyway? The Representation of the Older Child in Care Proceedings.* Thesis number DX188350. University of Sussex.

Cleaver, H. and Freeman, P. (1995) *Parental Perspectives in Cases of Suspected Child Abuse.* HMSO.

Coopersmith, (1967) *The Antecedents of Self-esteem.* San Fransisco, Freeman and Co.

Corrigan, M. (1996) *Listening to Children.* Pack.

Davey, A.G. (1987) Insiders, Outsiders and Anomalies: A Review Study of Identities. *New Community* 13, Spring.

Davies, G., Stevenson-Rob, Y. and Flin, R. (1986) The Reliability of Children's Testimony. *International Legal Practitioner.*

Dent, H. and Flin, R. (1992) *Children as Witnesses.* Chichester, Wiley.

Department of Health (1991) *The Children Act (1989) Guidance and Regulations Volume 4.* HMSO.

Department of Health (1995) National Standards for the Guardian ad litem and Reporting Officer Service. Department of Health.

Department of Health (1997) *Responding to Families in Need: The Inspection of Assessment, Planning and Decision Making in Family Support Services.* HMSO.

Department of Health (1999). *Modernising Health and Social Services, National Priorities Guidance*. London, DoH.

Department of Health (2000) *Framework for Assessment. of Children in Need and their Families*. HMSO.

Department of Health and OFSTED (1995). *The Education of Children who are Looked After by Local Authorities*, Department of Health and OFSTED.

Department of Health (1995) *Child Protection: Messages from Research*. HMSO.

Dutt, R. (1998) Knowing When to Move on. *Community Care*. 20–26 August.

Feltham, H. *How do Children Panel Solicitors Ascertain the Wishes and Feelings of their Child Clients in Public Law Proceedings*. unpublished MA Thesis.

Fitts, P. (1998) *The New Managerial Mentor*. Davies Black.

Fortin, J. (1998) *Children's Rights and the Developing Law*. Butterworth.

Freeman, M. (1994) Whither children: protection, participation, autonomy? *Seen and Heard*. Vol. 4.

Gaber, I. and Aldridge, J. (1994) *Culture, Identity and Trans-racial Adoption: In the Best Interests of the Child*. London, Free Association Books.

Gibbons, J., Conroy, S. and Bell, C. (1995) *Operating the Child Protection System: A study of Child Protection Practices in England and Wales*. HMSO.

Gill, and Jackson, (1983) *Adoption and Race: Black and mixed Race Children in White Families* London, Basford.

Gilroy, P. (1993) *Small Acts: Thoughts on the Politics of Black Cultures*. London, Serpents Tail.

Hayes, M. (1987) Placing Black Children. *Adoption and Fostering* 11: 3.

Hazel Mill Toys Ltd. (1998) *Make a Scene*. Hazel Mill Toys Ltd.

Hemmings, P. (1991) *All about Me*. Board game, Banardos.

Hertfordshire Panel of Guardian ad litem and Reporting Officers. *Guardian Service Calendar*.

HMSO (1989) *The Children Act*. London, HMSO.

HMSO (1998) *The Human Rights Act*. HMSO.

Howe, D. (1998) *Patterns of Adoption*. Oxford, Blackwell.

Howe, D. and Feast, J. (2000) *Adoption, Search and Reunion: The Long-term Experience of Adopted Adults*. London, The Children's Society.

Hughes, J. (2000) Implications for Guardians ad litem of the Stephen Lawrence Inquiry and Macpherson Report. *Seen and Heard*. 10: (1).

Hunt, I. and Murch, M. (1990) *Speaking out for Children*. The Children's Society.

Ince, L. (1998) *Making it Alone, A Study of the Care Experiences of Young Black People*. London, BAAF.

Jackson, S. (1987) *The Education of Children in Care*. Bristol. Bristol University, School of Applied Social Studies.

Johnson, P. and Sherman, J. (1987) Trans-racial Adoption and the Development of Black Identity at Age Eight. *Child Welfare*. 66.

Katz, I. (1996) *The Construction of Racial Identity of Children of Mixed Parentage: Mixed Metaphors*. London, Cromwell Press.

King and Young (1992) The Child as Client. *Family Law*.

King, J. (1993) Love is not Enough. *Community Care*. 12 August.

Kirton, D. (2000) *'Race', Ethnicity and Adoption*. Buckingham, Open University Press.

Laurance, J. (1983) Should White Families Adopt Black Children? *New Society*. 64.

Local Authority Circular (1998) *Adoption: Achieving the Right Balance*. 28th August.

Macpherson, Sir W. (1999) *The Stephen Lawrence Inquiry: Report of an Inquiry by Sir William Macpherson of Clury*. Stationery Office.

Masson, J. and Oakley, M. W. (1999) *Out of Hearing: The Representation by Guardians and Solicitors in Public Law Proceedings.* Wiley.

Mc Adoo, and Mc Adoo, (1985) *Black Children.* California, Sage.

McCausland, J. (2000) *Guarding Children's Interests: The Contribution of Guardians ad litem in Court Proceedings.* The Children's Society.

McRoy, and Zurcher, (1983) *Trans-racial and In-racial Adoptees. The Adolescent Years.* Springfield, Charles Thomas.

Moore, C. and Lane, M. (1992) *Meeting Your Guardian ad litem.* The Children's Society.

National Foster Care Association *My Book About Me.* NFCA.

Parker, E. and Farmer, R. (1991) *Trials and Tribulations: Returning Children from Care to their Families.* HMSO.

Pedlar, Burgoyne, and Boydell, (1991) *The Learning Company.* New York, McGraw-Hill.

Pennie, P. (1987) Black Children Need the Richness of Black Family Life. *Social Work.*

Piper, C. (1999) The Wishes and Feelings of the Child in Day, Slater and Piper (Eds.) *Undercurrents of Divorce.*

Ruegger, M. (2001) Seen and Heard but How Well Informed: Children's Perceptions of the Guardian Service. *Children and Society Journal.*

Ruegger, M. (2000) The Challenge of Meaningful and Purposeful Partnership with Parents whose Children are the Subjects of Public Law Proceedings: Balancing Independence with Empathy. in Wheal, A. (Ed.) *Working with Parents.* Lyme Regis, Russell House Publishing.

Ruxton, S. (1998) *Implementing Children's Rights: What Can the UK Learn from International Experience?* London, Save the Children.

Sawyer, C. (1995) *The Rise and Fall of the Third Party: Solicitors Assessments of the Competence of Children to Participate in Family Proceedings.* Centre for Socio-legal Studies, Wolfson College, University of Oxford.

Sawyer, C. (2000) *Rules Roles and Relationships: The Structure and Function of Child Representation and Welfare Within Family Proceedings.* Centre for Socio-legal Studies, Wolfson College, University of Oxford.

Schofield, G. (1998) Making Sense of the Ascertainable Wishes and Feelings of Insecurely Attached Children. *Child and Family Law Quarterly.* 10: 4.

Simon, R. J. and Alstein, H. (1987) *Trans-racial Adoptees and their Families.* New York, Praeger Press.

Small, (1986) in Ahmed, S. *et al. Social Work with Black Children and Their Families.* London, Batsford.

Social Exclusion Unit (1998) *Truancy and Social Exclusion.* Cm. 3957, Social Exclusion Unit.

Social Services Inspectorate (!999) *Getting Family Support Right.* London, Department of Health.

Solicitors Family law Association (2000) *Guide to Good Practice for Solicitors Acting for Children* (5th edn.). Solicitors Family law Association.

Spencer, and Markstrom-Adams, (1990) Identity Processes Among Racial and Ethnic Minority Children in America. *Child Development.* 61.

Spencer, M. *et al.* (1985) *Beginings: The Social and Affective Development of Black Children.* New Jersey, Lawrence Erlbaum.

Stein, M. (1989) Leaving Care. in Kahan, B. (Ed.) *Child Care Research Policy and Practice.* Hodder and Stoughton.

Stubbs, P. (1987) Professionalism and the Adoption of Black Children. *British Journal of Social Work*. 17.

Thoburn, J. and Sellick, C. (1996) *What Works in Family Placement?* Essex, Barnados.

Thoburn, J., Norford, L. and Rashid (1999) Permanent Family Placement for Children of Minority Ethnic Origin. in *Adoption Now, Messages from Reseach*. Chichester, John Wiley and Sons.

Timms, J. (1992) *The Manual of Practice Guidance for Guardians ad litem and Reporting Officers*. Department of Health.

Tizzard, and Phoenix, (1989) Black Identity and Trans-racial Adoption. *New Community*. 15 (3).

Tosey, P. (2000) Making Sense of Interventions: Stranger in a Strange Land. in Wheal, A. (Ed.) *Working with Parents*. Lyme Regis, Russell House Publishing.

Utting, Sir W. (1991) *Children in Public Care: A Review of Residential Care*. HMSO.

Vizard, E. (1991) Interviewing Children Suspected of Being Sexually Abused: A review of Theory and Practice. in Hollin, C. R. and Howells, K. (Eds.) *Clinical Approaches to Sex Offenders and their Victims*.

Waterhouse, S. (1987) *Time for Me*. a resource book.

Wedge, and Phelan, (1987) The Impossible Demands of Children.

Wheal, A. (1994). Working with Children. *Seen and Heard*. 4: 22–3.